Meditations on Sufism

The Way of the Modern Darvish

ARSALAN MOZAFFARI FALARTI

BALBOA.
PRESS
A DIVISION OF HAY HOUSE

Balboa Press books may be ordered through booksellers or by contacting:

Balboa Press
A Division of Hay House
1663 Liberty Drive
Bloomington, IN 47403
www.balboapress.com.au
1-(877) 407-4847

ISBN: 978-1-4525-0658-6 (sc)
ISBN: 978-1-4525-0657-9 (hc)
ISBN: 978-1-4525-0659-3 (e)

Library of Congress Control Number: 2012913889

Because of the dynamic nature of the Internet, any web addresses or links contained in this book may have changed since publication and may no longer be valid. The views expressed in this work are solely those of the author and do not necessarily reflect the views of the publisher, and the publisher hereby disclaims any responsibility for them.

The author of this book does not dispense medical advice or prescribe the use of any technique as a form of treatment for physical, emotional, or medical problems without the advice of a physician, either directly or indirectly. The intent of the author is only to offer information of a general nature to help you in your quest for emotional and spiritual well-being. In the event you use any of the information in this book for yourself, which is your constitutional right, the author and the publisher assume no responsibility for your actions.

Cover Image by Julieanne Hupalo

Printed in the United States of America

Balboa Press rev. date: 09/04/2012

جمله معشوق است و عاشق پرده ای

Beloved is all, lover is a veil,

زنده معشوق است و عاشق مرده ای

Beloved is the alive, lover is the dead

ACKNOWLEDGMENTS

Conventions

The author deeply respects and appreciates that readers will be of both genders and wishes no disrespect to female readers by the choice in editing to use conventional male pronouns in this English publication. In the original Farsi draft a neutral pronoun meaning "his or her" and "he or she" was utilized.

The author also wishes for readers to appreciate the use of traditional words and phrases within the Nematollahi Ghadeer Ali Shahi Sufi Order. It is accepted that Sufism is monotheistic and as such the names for this one God encompass Hagh, Ahura Mazda, Allah, Jehovah, God, Yazdaan, Yahweh, The Beloved, Creator, and will be referenced within this text. Hagh is used predominantly due to the traditions of this Order.

The author has included the names of traditional Sufi mystic writers at the end of this book, if the reader to assist the reader in expanding their knowledge of the topics covered.

جمله معشوق است و عاشق پرده ای

CONTENTS

جمله معشوق است و عاشق پرده ای

جمله معشوق است و عاشق پرده ای

HUMANITY WANTS LOVE AND NOT HATRED.

A Darvish, also known as a Sufi, has both historically and at the present time been respected and regarded to be an example and a representative for love, indigence, honesty, honour, meekness, humbleness, sincerity and simplicity. His nature is to be calm, tranquil and quiet and he appears either to live in abject poverty or to have no attachment to those few possessions he may have.

From the earliest times where Darvishes resided in a society, the society agreed (and still agrees) that Darvishes render pure and heartfelt love to all people regardless of their physical appearance, race, caste, religion, ideology, belief, education, wealth, prestige or lack thereof. Darvishes offer love out of their sincere and pure hearts. It is not a "love" that has been decided upon by their minds.

At the present time, in both the Eastern and Western world, not only do Darvishes enjoy the reputation they enjoyed in the past (particularly in the East), furthermore are also well recognised and received internationally. This is because they bestow and distribute love equally to all and freely and sincerely offer that everywhere, wherever they may be, wherever people need to be loved.

Currently unpleasant and disturbing news is distributed much faster than any other newsworthy events. Stories about dishonesty, hatred, cheating, stealing, corruption, killings and all other improper actions and behaviours of some individuals are broadcast in real time, even before evil action is finished.

Human beings listen to the news or watch or read about them and become worried, sad and unhappy because of them. Humanity wants LOVE and not Hatred.

Man is thirsty for true love and indigence. The hearts of all humans are tired of darkness and all of the wrong actions.

Under such hard and confusing situations and conditions, a Darvish feels responsible to offer love and purity, without expectation of any reward or exchange.

جمله معشوق است و عاشق پرده ای

1

درویش

DARVISH

A LITTLE KNOWLEDGE IS DANGEROUS

So called "modern man" is facing lots of different types and forms of brain, nerve and life pressures e.g. emotional, psychological, financial, physical, cultural and social. These factors act upon him whether directly by those perpetrating acts upon him or indirectly by witnessing it e.g. via news reportage. The citizen of the modern world suffers from depression, anxiety, sadness, tiredness, unhappiness, heavy pressure on the mind, worries and insecurity. This unhappy person is tired from the poor quality of his life, therefore seeks to find a simple, easy and workable cure for his unhappy, sick and troubled situation. This modern man looks not just for a solution but for *THE* meaningful and achievable solution to the problems of his daily life and most importantly, a simple to understand, easy to practice, not materially expensive and practical solution.

Usually such a hopeful, eager, willing and interested person, in order to find a definite medicine for his illness, searches, tries and examines lots of different ways, methods, systems, and opinions. He may even in some cases feel that he has to try different kinds of drugs and intoxicating materials. In spite of all of his hopes these paths will not give him any cure or lasting satisfaction.

This confused person, during his attempts, may also come across the teachings of the school of Darvish-hood or Sufism and conclude that the solution is here in this Maktab—school.

The person may hope and believe that the simple but meaningful method of life the old Persian Darvish philosophers and knowledgeable people had, still have and follow, could be practical and beneficial to him. He may believe that the teachings of this School can be, if not "The One", at least one of the best solutions for his problems, and be the cure to his sickness.

On the above basis he therefore decides to get more information about Sufism and a Darvish's simple way of life, hoping that this Path can be the practical and the

جمله معشوق است و عاشق پرده ای

most promising solution to all or the greater part of his difficulties, problems and hard times that he is currently experiencing.

With high hope and expectation the modern man shows more and more interest in this Path and the purity and simplicity of the teachings of this school. He may begin to study the doctrine, ethics and ideology of the school with more and more interest, attention, seriousness and a great deal of hope. He will do his best to gather more information and knowledge about this Darvish way of life, hoping that by the help and guidance, and through following the teachings of this school he also may gain back true happiness, tranquility and peace.

In Iran, and also other parts of neighboring countries, pure, innocent and sincere foundations of this Maktab—School—of Darvish-hood or Sufism exist. These foundations date back thousands of years and not as some people think only during the last ten or fifteen centuries. Love and pure feelings were already bestowed on Man at the time of Creation and not yesterday or today. It has always been there. If Man cannot feel or see it, it is his own fault.

Sincere Darvishes still travel around the world to learn more and to gladly offer and teach these facts when and where it is necessary and required, or asked from them.

Darvishes without expectation of being recognised or rewarded continue to serve members of their society to the best of their ability. The reward for a Darvish is the happiness of the receiver of their service and teachings.

The source of whatever a Darvish offers and does in society is the love in his heart; this directs his wish to serve. Darvishes trust that the heartfelt, sincere love is always well accepted and respected.

Generally, the loving service the Darvishes render receives recognition, warm respect and admiration from society. The Darvish devotional method of life is well appreciated and happily welcomed by most people. People hope they themselves may one day become relieved from all the troubles of their present life and be content, meek and simply happy, giving, serving and relaxed like the Darvish is.

Darvishes or Sufis, similar to other socially respected and accepted serving societies or groups, are well received, generally speaking. Of course, it is inevitable that this

جمله معشوق است و عاشق پرده ای

school of devotion and sincerity, as are all other people or organizations, faces some envy or jealousy by some who have different desires, thoughts, expectations, wishes and ideas. Such a mentality and way of thinking is inevitable, it has been, is, and will continue to be as such, therefore is understandable and acceptable to Darvishes.

There are groups of people who are fanatically devoted to their own opinions so they prejudge. These people decide to get more information so as to use that information against the Path. Darvishes have been and still are under question and/or the suspicion of some individuals or groups. This mentality is also understandable and acceptable to Darvishes as they are servants and are living to serve, so it doesn't bother or worry them.

However, aside from the disparagers, there are also another group of people, the people who sincerely and truly are interested and wish to know more about Darvishes and are willing to learn more about their beliefs, hopes and ethics.

Darvishes respectfully accept the mentality and opinion of these different groups of people. Darvishes accept it because they all have a limited amount of knowledge or information about the Maktab—School—of Sufism, and a little knowledge is not sufficient or practical to enlighten. You may have heard the proverb that says:

A little knowledge is a dangerous (or poisonous) thing.

Most of those aforementioned people are intelligent and generally good hearted. They are people who are eager to learn more and to know more about the Darvish's path, life, ideas and code of ethics. These people have so many questions in their mind which they believe, by seeking the answers, will assist and serve their purpose; hoping that this will help them to find and choose the proper path and method for a happy and griefless life for themselves. The questions these innocent, interested people ask are primarily to help them learn and understand.

THE SIMPLE ANSWER . . . .

Those groups, with their variety of motivations for knowledge, intend to get more information about the Path, its teachings, the practicality and what a person will achieve from following those teaching and ethics of the Path.

The simple answer to all of their questions is:

Darvishes are proud of being at the service of all, rendering sincere heartfelt service to all, whoever needs it. Darvishes do not see any colour, nationality, religion, belief, rationale and/or politic. Darvishes understand and recognise that all are human beings are created by our Most Beloved Darling God (Hagh).

Darvish's sincerity has been recognised throughout history, and is well accepted by societies and the opinion of the people. In the past, when people talked about Darvishes or Sufis and the Darvish way of life, the judgment for the most part has been in favour of their sincerity, meekness, their heartfelt services, their belief and their spiritual Path of Love.

This opinion exists, if not held in higher esteem and more positive, to this day.

Neutral honest people agree that Darvishes and the followers of this school and Path are not desirous or interested in gaining social recognition and respect, material achievement, worldly recognition, or even any type of reward. On the contrary, they are after the opportunity to serve human society in all aspects.

Particularly, Darvishes or Sufis wish to have the blessing to serve those who need more service, assistance and help. As a result the society in which a Darvish lives hold positive and respectful opinions of the service, respect, love and devotion this Darvish has towards the life in that society.

A Darvish loves respects and serves all Creation. Love has no limits or barriers. Love does not stop here or there or anywhere.

جمله معشوق است و عاشق پرده ای

HAGH

LOVE IS ETERNAL, FROM ETERNITY TO ETERNITY.

The Golden rule for Darvishes or Sufis in general is very simple and easy to understand. A follower of the teachings of the school of Sufism is to conduct his life according to these rules:

- ❖ Control your actions by using your mind

- ❖ Control your mind by using your wisdom

- ❖ Ensure your wisdom is gained through the guidance of love from your sincere HEART

The heart is the sacred repository and temple for the love of God, the Most High, the Most Glorious Beneficent and Merciful Beloved of all.

That is all.

Yaa Hagh

جمله معشوق است و عاشق پرده ای

SEYR (EVOLUTION)

Seyr and Solook are the two wings that help a person to fly high out of the material and mortal world to everlasting life; one without the other will not be strong enough to keep the person on their way.

SEYR is a Darvish's inward advancement towards perfection, purity and quality of life. The quality that directs, governs and controls his thoughts, actions, behaviors, feelings, judgments, hopes and desires. Seyr is what persuades and directs people to do what is right, prepares devotees to love the whole of Creation, to have positive feelings, creative decisions, non—judgmental and fruitful thoughts, honest desires, and logical hopes.

SOLOOK—Behaviour—directs the Darvish to control his outward or social manners, behaviour, and services by love, devotion, sincerity and honesty. Solook may be interpreted as the outward reflections and consequences of the inward processes or Seyr.

Evolution—Seyr—is the spiritual and heartfelt advancement a Darvish makes in his life. This progress polishes his heart to lustre, which purifies his mind gradually and accordingly that in its turn controls and directs his thoughts. The thoughts in their turn will transfer into actions; private and personal, outward, social actions and behaviors.

This continuation and connection is what Zoroaster, according to many the first Monotheist prophet of God, declared as:

GOOD THOUGHTS, GOOD WORDS, GOOD DEEDS.

Improvement and advancement of the thoughts and the consequent actions by the person takes place continually and gradually during the course of his lifetime, which highly depends upon the capacity of that person's heart, the amount of wisdom and knowledge a person has gathered during his life and the capacity and

جمله معشوق است و عاشق پرده ای

obedience of his mind. It must not be forgotten or ignored that nothing important, either constructive and/or destructive can or will happen overnight, without practice and exercise. It takes time.

One of the major factors for a Darvish to advance to a higher heartfelt and spiritual level in many cases depends on his endeavour, through his devotion, sincere obedience and cooperation with his teacher or Master.

The advancement of a Darvish in all aspects of life, through all stages of Darvish-hood from the early and primary stages to the point of becoming a Master himself, is decided, directed, guided, and corrected by his Master. The first positive step forward in this training is the fact the Darvish has steadfast faith, is truthful, positive, productive and has sincere intentions, obeys and follows his heart which is already guided by Love; this preparation of the mind for following the heart prepares the Darvish to give his Service to anyone who needs it.

To start travelling in the path of love and devotion, to wear the garb of Service, to break the ugly crust of ego and selfishness, to taste and practice meekness, to control passion and to direct instincts in the proper direction, to elevate and advance to the highest level of human values, to fly high towards the position of a true COMPLETE MAN, to brighten the heart and purify the mind, to become a true and real person worthy to be called a human, a loving and amorous person who is worthy enough for this title and to be accepted and completely dissolved in his Beloved, the Darvish has to surrender completely and fully all material and physical expectations, he has to grow out of his ego, erase self-centring, control his desires, passion and wishes; he has to die out of his "I" and his selfish being so that he may be born in a pure innocent serving life and live in Hagh.

A person with the qualities as above is entitled to be addressed as a meek and indigent Darvish.

A Darvish, in order to become in all aspects capable and worthy enough to fly high to the elevated and holy position of a true and real human, has to have and benefit from two healthy and strong, powerful, obedient and faultless wings. Those two wings are his "Seyr va Solook"-Evolution and Proper Behaviour. To succeed in reaching the highest position and to gain the achievements of what a person's

جمله معشوق است و عاشق پرده ای

high goals are, those two wings have to grow simultaneously, healthy, strong, powerful, humble, obedient and equally; those two wings have to work completely in harmony with each other and together serve the person's purpose successfully and as expected of them.

In case a person has at his service only one of those two wings, no matter how it may look to be healthy, strong and reliable or the person thinks that only one is dependable, powerful, healthy and reliable, it will not be sufficient and efficient enough to serve the purpose of advancement, improvement and flying high.

To a bird one wing alone is not good enough and is not reliable to fly high, even if it seems to be strong enough on the ground. Flying high and over long distances, one wing cannot do the job of two wings. On the same basis, for a disciple of Sufism, concentration on only one quality either Seyr (Evolution) or Solook (Behaviour) would not be sufficient to help to ascend higher.

The person who is pure and innocent in his Seyr and is sincere and kind in rendering service and dealing with other creatures (Solook) is the person who may be referred to as THE COMPLETE MAN.

How would a bird look to be A Complete Bird or can be considered as a healthy bird with only one of the wings grown naturally and to the normal size while the other wing immature and incomplete? That is unusual and imperfect and the bird itself is not a complete bird. Similarly, if or when a Darvish concentrates on one of those two qualities and ignores the other his situation is similarly incomplete, he still will not be capable to fly to higher horizons he is expected to.

در گردا گرد و گیر اگیر نار احتی دست و پا میزدم که به ناگهان مجذوب انوار دلنشین عشق حضرت حق شدم ,

از احساس و دریافت تابش آن انوار دل من روشنی گرفت , و روح من به اسرار حضرت حق وقوف یافت.

درک این سخن سخت مینماید , لیک , بدان نا ممکن نیست , که به حقیقت از عنایت حضرت حق است به سالک از خویش رسته و کوشائی او که او را به این چنان مقامی ارتقا دهند. مقام فنا

یا حق

Gladly in the middle of struggle and discontent,

The pleasant rupture of his love absorbed me,

The shining rays of Hagh enlightened my heart,

My soul thus became aware of Hagh secrets.

All explained above appear to be hard, but not impossible.

By Hagh's guidance sincere wayfarer will arrive to the station of FANA

Yaa Hagh

Hazrate Ghadeer Ali Shah.

There may be exceptions of course—What? Where? When? How? Only HAGH Knows and decides.

It should not be ignored that in our human standard and normal laws of nature and life it is a fact that to concentrate on practicing evolution or behaviour singly, is still a positive action and has good influence in the person's life and manners. In its capacity it brings positive results but to serve the purpose of serving HAGH thoroughly it is not sufficient, as in the case of the bird it does not serve a person to become a complete Man. Laws of nature do not just "happen" they are following and obeying natural laws that have been designed for them from the very beginning.

جمله معشوق است و عاشق پرده ای

A Darvish has to grow and develop in both divisions of Seyr va Solook—Evolution and behaviour. Sufism gradually, continuously and according to the capacity of the heart and mind of a Darvish helps and trains him to progress in both qualities.

Sufism guides, directs, assists, trains and helps the Darvish to develop from within, with the proper method suiting his capacity, condition and ability. Thus he will succeed in his journey in the Path of love, of devotion, of giving, of non-existence, or in general; the direction to The Truth at his own pace and blessed by The Most Glorious and Most High.

جمله معشوق است و عاشق پرده ای

SOLOOK (BEHAVIOUR)

A Darvish has two important departments to develop in life, the inward and outward or SEYR and SOLOOK.

A Darvish is expected by the Maktab e Tasavvof—The school of Sufism—to be a sincere and positively active member of his society. On this holy basis the devoted person feels that he has to confirm and prove this fact by actions and not only claim it by words. The Darvish lives in society amongst the people in that society. He mixes with people and joins them in all of their social activities that he can or he may attend i.e. he joins in all of the respectable activities, services and honest jobs in his society.

The great Darvishes, Sufi Masters and Gnostic Teachers have described this important expectation, principal and foundational part of Darvish life as his SOLOOK (behaviour). Solook may be described as the Darvish's behaviour and manner but includes the relationship of the Darvish to the whole world in general and to the members of the society amongst whom he resides and lives, in particular. To explain this point further, the Darvish is expected to be physically in the society, with the people; working, serving, eating, praying, acting, giving, granting, sleeping, forgiving and forgetting other people's misbehaviour towards him. The Darvish is an obedient citizen of the world as he loves the world, which is created in love by his Beloved Hagh.

A Darvish, in order to be able to thoroughly and positively serve his society in the best way possible, must educate himself to understand his society's qualities and particulars much deeper than any ordinary member of that society may do. Knowledge about the society and of its needs is the first step for the interested person to help and serve, Darvish or not, as this is most important and vital. To perform their duties Darvishes not only have to observe and consider whatever all people have to observe, but they are to seriously consider this as a Godly duty, a duty to be performed with heartfelt happiness and joyfulness.

جمله معشوق است و عاشق پرده ای

نوری گفت : از عزلت بپرهیزید که آن مقارنت شیطان است و بر شـما باد

به صحبت که در صحبت خشنودی

خدای عز و جل اسـت

Avoid seclusion, since it is associating with the Devil,

Be to you the companionship of people,

since that enjoys pleasure and happiness of God.

Abolhasan e Noori,Sufi Master of the third century A. H.

To render a positive, right and proper service not only for a Darvish but for all of those members who wish to serve their society, it is vital to investigate and study the system, mentality, culture, wisdom, spirituality, financial situation, health and educational level of their society. A person who does not know what their society is like and what the needs and requirements are of that society cannot provide a positive constructive service that is the best for that society. How can he? A Darvish lives a physical life similar to all of the other people; however his heart and mind are completely with his most Beloved and Creator, Hagh, thus he conducts all of the above mentioned life and actions according to his moralities and for Hagh. From eternity to eternity is created by Hagh in His love and a Darvish is an obedient devoted slave in and for the Love of Hagh; he is entirely at the service of Creation without asking any questions, or rejecting any case or person when his heart feels that his service is required.

The duty of a Darvish is to lovingly, kindly and with positive intention point out whatever he has observed and found to be improper, unjust, wrong, or jeopardizing to even the smallest member of the whole of Creation. Beyond this, the Darvish must find the illness of society and assist in finding the cure. It is vital that Darvishes or Sufis, with love, sincerity, truthfulness and devotion point out the mistake, recommend and offer the proper and correct way to cure the sickness, and as necessary have their "sleeves up" to get into the correction. They should also help, assist and direct other people to understand the meaning, the good and productive reasons surrounding those aims and the best method to make it possible for the society to obtain those qualities. The Darvish feels bound by obligation to provide the service at the best of his capacity and ability—Sufis do not make promises they cannot keep. They are well prepared, if necessary, to sacrifice their own life to serve society and to help people in true and real need for their help.

A Darvish believes that he has no right for reward, respect, recognition, wage, or anything in exchange for the service he renders. The Darvish believes that he already has received whatever capacity, ability, heartfelt feeling, intelligence and wisdom in his possession free and from Love, so by the same token he feels happy and obliged to give freely and out of love. The Darvish's role in serving others is similar to the role of a waiter—just serving, without asking any questions. A person who has registered in the Maktab e Tasavvof, but does not observe the above vital points should think twice and change his manners accordingly.

جمله معشوق است و عاشق پرده ای

Gnostics refer to this aspect of Darvish life as:

سلوک درویش در رابطه با خلق

Darvish's behave towards people (SOLOOK).

However Solook is not just a Darvish's relation with the world outside him; it includes the Darvish's relationship with himself. His respect and service towards himself, the honesty and sincerity he shows to himself, his intention for stopping, preventing and not allowing his Devil (his mind) to fool him while working upon the perfection of his material life. This part of the life of the Darvish in Sufism is called Solook e baa khod (Behaviour towards self).

Solook to a Darvish means to live in society, with the people, to serve the people, to work with the people and to have a normal life together with them, while his heart and mind is completely devoted to Hagh. The Darvish lives in the society while his intention is to serve and help other people to the best of his ability because Hagh has granted him all of the abilities he is enjoying. By all of his effort and power he obeys Hagh—TRUTH. In all of his actions his intention is service, service and service; he also eagerly and happily tries to help and direct other people to find the road to Hagh. He invites his fellow humans to join him in the joy that exists in sincere service.

HE WHO IS NOT A SINCERE SERVANT IS NOT A DARVISH.

A Darvish is to *serve* and *serve*; serve without any expectation of recognition, respect or reward in exchange for his service.

One of Great masters accompanied by a number of his disciples was visiting a cemetery when they saw a skull. On the forehead of the skull had been written:

"THE LOSER OF THIS AND THE COMING WORLD"

The Master picked up the skull, cleaned the dust from it and kissed it. The disciples were astonished and asked him the reason for such respect to the skull and the Master, while smiling, replied; "This person has been a Darvish, had no desire for the glories of this world and no expectation for the happiness of rewards of the next world. This indigent person merely served people."

That great rule or teaching in the Path can simply by explained by one word or maxim and that is:

SERVE

Some curious and interested people wish to learn more about the mentality, works, services, ethics and lifestyle of Darvishes. They also wish to find out if the stories attributed to Darvishes, by either a simple advocate, lovers or slanderers are true or false? Those people wish to know more about the strange and extraordinary performances and the miracles claimed to be performed by Darvishes. Are the stories true or exaggeration?

The simplest answer of course, surely and definitely in the past, now and into the future is that Darvishes make miracles. The most glorious and extraordinary miracle of any Darvish is his intention of self-denial and sincere SERVICE. Can there be any MIRACLE greater than this?

جمله معشوق است و عاشق پرده ای

Please consider the act of controlling and holding back egoistic desires, passions, expectations, the wishes and the wants of instincts, keeping them under the full and complete control of the heart. Surely this is a miracle.

The hope and intention of Maktab e Tasavvof—The School of Sufism—is to refine, treat, purify, change and improve the thoughts of the mind of devotees and disciples towards the Path of Love and Devotion, which in turn will direct, control and improve their consequent thoughts, conducts, actions and behaviour.

The above goal cannot be achieved unless the feelings and thoughts are purified and directed towards truth and sincerity. Through the teaching, training and guidelines of the school, disciples are helped, assisted and guided to purify their thoughts and direct their behaviour and conduct to the right and proper direction. The disciples learn the correct method and practice of directing and adapting the right way to control and eliminate improper thoughts and consequent actions and to change them into right and appropriate ones. This process and method of advancement and improvement may be described as:

- ❖ follow the direction recommended by the heartfelt love

- ❖ control the ego wisely

- ❖ control the passion properly

- ❖ control the desires and expectations seriously

HAPPINESS IS HERE IN THE HEART OF EACH
AND EVERY HUMAN

The mission of the Maktab e Tasavvof is to direct, train, teach and persuade people to create as much healthy, logical permanent happiness and satisfaction as practically possible for themselves, their family, their neighbour and the human society in general. The duty of this school is to teach and direct individuals as well as societies to believe that true happiness exists. This true happiness does not live outside the person, here, there or who knows where. To achieve true happiness and tranquility it is up to the individuals in particular and the societies in general to search inside themselves, surely they will find it there, as it is already there but covered with the desires of ego, worldly wants and uncontrolled instincts.

The school directs the disciples to respect and highly value the life of other creatures as being as equally valuable as their own. To a truly devoted Darvish, the interests and rights of all other people and creatures in Creation must be as valuable and equal to his own. A Darvish seizes the control of his life from egoistic desires and passions and submits total control of his actions to the Love from his heart. This is the hardest practice and is the greatest miracle a Darvish performs.

When people are sincere and meek they will feel internal peace, tranquility and happiness. When one is not greedy there is no reason for him not to be relaxed, if a person is not corrupt, then why should he be afraid of law, investigation, and punishment or being afraid of his superiors?

A Darvish believes that people are content, happy, successful, calm and relaxed and can make right judgments when their life is conducted through their heartfelt love.

True Darvishes not only talk, they act and they work hard to direct other people to the right path; the path of love, peace and devotion. Darvishes hope to not only persuade others to believe in honesty and sincerity but to practice honesty and sincerity.

جمله معشوق است و عاشق پرده ای

A Darvish feels this truth within and loves to discuss it, to convince others to understand this simple truth. A Darvish wishes others to feel real happiness, understanding that it is not in what they possess, but on the contrary, happiness depends on their own intention and how they accept the possibilities, abilities, wealth or qualities that have been given and granted to them even before entering this world. When people sincerely accept this they will find that what they have is enough to make them happy and satisfied with life; however the first step is that they must intend to and want to see it. Happiness does not come from outside, happiness does not come from anywhere else; happiness is already here inside Man, all that is required is that he must observe and enjoy.

Search for happiness inside your hearts, it is here, not on the distant horizon, it is here in you and all around you.

The intention of Darvish Masters has always been to teach this undeniable fact to their disciples. Peace and happiness is not in another unreachable world, on another planet, a world far away and untouchable, neither is it an unobtainable fantasy.

Happiness is here in the heart of each and every human. For the mind and the ego to understand this great reality one must only surrender to the feelings of the heart.

هرکه چهار چیز بدانست از چهار چیز برست:

Whoever observes four points, will be saved from four dangers.

هر که بدانست که خدای تعالی در آفرینش غلط نکرده است , از عیب برست

Whoever believes Allah Most high has made no mistake
in His Creation, is saved from faults.

هرکه بدانست که هرچه قضا ست بدو خواهد رسید , از غم برست.

Whoever believes he will receive whatever is destined from him,
he is saved from grief

و هر که بدانست که در قسمت میل نکرده است , از حسد برست

And whoever accepts that he has had no say in his destiny,
will be saved from jealousy.

و هر که بدانست که اصل او از چیست , از تکبر برست

And whoever considers what and where from his origin is
(Clay), will be saved from pride.

Khajeh Abdollah

RELIGIONS

All Godly religions are to help to save Man from his materialistic and worldly burdens. Those holy religions normally possess their own form and/or system and method of supplications and prayers in order to purify thoughts and behaviour. To assist the determination of their followers the religions may persuade their believers to pray in temples, synagogues, churches and mosques as much as they can; may order fasting, or recommend pilgrimages to holy places. The pilgrimage assists the believers in many ways: it gets them away from their home so they may have their minds away from their daily affairs; where they also may meet their fellow believers from around the world, get to know each other, learn about each other's life conditions and help each other if needed.

Religion by its laws, regulations and duties designated for its followers promises to them that it will help, assist, direct and guide them to have a pure, happy and safe life here in this world as well as a fully pleasant and successful everlasting life in the life to come in the future. No one has ever come across any religion which teaches anything contrary to this doctrine. If some unacceptable and improper behaviour and action or idea is observed from anyone who claims to be the follower of any of the Godly religions, the observing person should not forget that it is not the fault of that religion but the fault is from the person or persons who CLAIM they are the followers of that religion.

A great number of the members of human society think that to follow their religion truly, is simply to obey the laws, external practices, or symbolic actions of that religion. Those people believe that simple observance of written rituals, performance of set ceremonies, and pilgrimages to the holy places which are recommended is all a religious person has to do and if he performed those things he will have his great palace with servants, all kinds of foods and drinks and everything in his imaginary paradise.

But surely we must ask: is that all we must do?

جمله معشوق است و عاشق پرده ای   23

To that sort of follower it is vital to say and perform prayers repeatedly and whenever they find time, to them it is extra achievement if they observe extra fasting in addition to the ones they are supposed to observe. They also make pilgrimages to holy and sacred places anytime they are able. Those people perform anything visible and practical to follow their religion in the proper way. Their actions are right and proper but are they the only true rules of religion?

Those religious people may be referred to as innocent people. They are completing and performing, not only at all of the times required whatever is expected of them according to the teaching of their religious clergies and leaders, but whenever they can. But when they do, they still are not completely happy or sure if they will receive their reward on the day of resurrection—will they receive the key to that inconceivable palace in paradise for which they have been labouring all of their mature life?

What a life! Is this the life their Creator decided for them: a life full of worry, labouring and hard work and not feeling completely calm and relaxed? They seem to be groping in the dark for evidence from God but God is not material or physical so that He may be completely sought for in this material world and with this physical body. Has The Glorious, Merciful, Almighty decided to create Man so that He may have someone in His possession to torture and punish? Is the reason for Man's Creation, to keep him in misery, agony, fear and unrest?

Moulana Rumi in his famous book of Masnavi has a very meaningful poem which is titled 'Moses and the Shepherd'. At the time of Moses, God's prophet, there was a shepherd herding his flock upon the mountains. He, in his simple, loving, peasant language and according to his heartfelt feelings and experience, was always talking to his creator God. His words were simple, sincere and full of heartfelt messages and promises to his Creator.

The shepherd invites God to his tiny, little shepherd hut and promises to serve Him and help Him to the best of his ability. He says:

"Where are you so your needs I can serve

Mend your shoes, your hair comb, curl and curve.

Wash your clothes, kill your lice, pick your nits

جمله معشوق است و عاشق پرده ای

Bring you milk, while your Majesty just sits.

Kiss your lovely hands, and rub your tiny feet

When it is time to sleep, sweep your room, make it neat.

For you I will sacrifice all my goats

Thinking of you I shout and sing my notes"

The shepherd continues his conversation, offering his simple, sincere offers and presentations as such. He is pleased since he is sure his Lord is pleased as well.

Moses, on his way to his sacred sanctuary to worship and talk to God hears him. To Moses it is all blasphemy and he cannot accept this so Moses rushes to the shepherd and very aggressively stops him and scolds him, explaining to the shepherd what a prophet has to explain.

Now the poor shepherd is sad and he is sorry and disappointed with himself because of all of those past years that he has been saying so much blasphemy. What to do? He bursts into tears, tears his clothes and dashes to the mountains out of sight.

Moses, maybe pleased with himself, continues to perform his daily prayers. After he finishes, God is not pleased with him and scolds him, but why?

Molavi explains in his poetic, mystic language so finely and beautifully how Jehovah scolds him because of his improper behaviour towards that poor shepherd. God tells Moses that he has hurt one of God's best friends and expresses as below:

ما نکرد یم خلق تا سود ی کسنیم

We did not create to make a profit

بلکه تا بر بند گان جسودی کنسیم

But to bestow munificence on creatures

جمله معشوق است و عاشق پرده ای   25

The Lord commands Moses to go find the shepherd apologise to him, bring him back to his little shepherd hut and give him the good news that his Creator is happy with his method and wants him to continue.

When a person reads the whole poem they will appreciate the detailed story of Moses with all the glory and holiness he had, the way of his thinking, the method he was considering as the proper method for respecting his Lord Jehovah. Then meeting and hearing the simple, uneducated peasant shepherd covered and immerged in his simplicity, sincerity, love and devotion to his most gorgeous beloved Creator, the reader will be amazed, will feel pure, will wish to fly with joyfulness and will see and appreciate the perfection in that simple man.

When comparing Moses' idea and opinion on praying to the Lord with the plain method the simple shepherd was practicing, and visualising Moses' anger and disappointment with the shepherd, and then Jehovah's disappointment with Moses, it will open the mind of Mankind to ask: what is he to do?

It appears that all external rites and forms are useful only in so far as they arouse the people's religious emotion, and instills in them the spirit of devotion, but does not travel further, it is not enough. Their talks and prayers do not guarantee the happiness of the Lord, their Creator.

In most cases those religious actions and simple obedience do not open the inner eyes of people and show them transcendent reality. For Mankind deeper, more sincere, more pure, and more humble service to all the other creatures through the heart is required to help them to wake Mankind up from the heavy sleep they are entangled in.

Of course all religions preach morality and induce people to tread in the footsteps of great personages; but their answers to spiritual and heartfelt fundamental questions are limited to lots of factors which are directly connected to the person, the way he has been taught and his expectations for the help he gives to others.

Man needs something closer to his heart and emotions, something to give him hope, love, happiness, to satisfy his inner feelings, and to save him from the burdens and material pressures which are continually pressing upon his heart, mind and nerves so harshly.

جمله معشوق است و عاشق پرده ای

The heart of Man is created to give and receive love, therefore does not agree with simply performing all of those prescribed laws and actions expected by some religious leaders, in exchange for the hope they give him—a paradise—the specifications, qualities, characteristics and overall picture of what is described and illustrated similar to what they have or wish or dream to have in this material world and life. Heaven is not a material, earthly product.

The heart of Man is the house of God, the house of his Glorious Creator, the place for love and devotion. The heart expects complete and sincere heartfelt actions of Man towards Creation, no matter who or what, be they Man, animal, plant, or even inanimate objects. The Qur'an says:

.... even inanimate praise God, you do not hear them ....

The true teaching of all religions is quite simple and easy: all of them want Mankind to love each other, serve each other, forgive each other, and act honestly and sincerely to each other, as well as adhering to all of the laws and regulations and religious actions. Simple prayers and actions of that kind do not do much good for the happiness of their followers, or for the satisfaction of the Creator.

Religion is not simply a material, worldly idea or thing that may be measured with the kinds of scales and weights used in this material world. A real religious person is a true lover of his Creator, feels nothing, thinks nothing, needs nothing, wants nothing, hopes for nothing, and expects nothing but only to feel, think, need, hope and expect the satisfaction and happiness of his Creator, the Beloved and the Most High. "Islam" means "to surrender". When a person surrenders what authority does he or she have to want, wish, expect and desire?

Such a devoted person must show his sincerity to the Most Beloved by serving all of His creatures without anything but love for Him. All religious activities come later; they are secondary.

Every ideology has its own constitution, inward and outward actions and reactions, attractions and rejections. The outward is in most cases attractive, bright, pleasant, and interesting and that is because appearance is what people come and pay attention to. Because exterior appearance is what attracts and absorbs some people they become interested and perhaps they conclude that they will be well off with that school of thought. However those people who are more interested and join

جمله معشوق است و عاشق پرده ای

do not know the interior practices, or the rigorous maxims by which the religion is governed. Many of those people will stop at this point as they were ignorant people who wanted easy things and are not active enough to work for the right path; they are the tasty and proper victims for sharks. Many so called masters who look for material worldly success and vast numbers of followers in order to satisfy their ego and receive their material needs do jump to fish, or that is to say, seize the opportunity and treacherously cheat the innocent and ignorant who are attracted to outward glamorous glitter. The dishonest or opportunistic people will fascinate and amuse them by outward bright and shiny shows, and keep them highly amused by false reflections, never giving them a chance to walk away, to think or try to know about the inward reality.

In reality those false masters are themselves shallow too; they have never been aware or know the inward, they know nothing about values, glory, love, integrity and dignity. They have always been outside the walls of sincerity and purity, truthfulness and honesty. These materialistic, and yet poor people, preach outside the walls of the castle of Love selling to the majority of their innocent audience an illusion or reflection which shines with glamour but remains outside of truth and reality. It is easier to see and be excited by those masters who sell to those interested but ignorant people their own imagination and visions painted in the colours of glitter.

Their audience, in the majority, is happy with those colours, music, words and the overall outward attractions but there is a minority who realise that what is being presented does not have any considerable value for them as a devotee. These dissatisfied people sincerely wish to be devotees, are the people who have answered the invitation and have come to surrender their material existence and become purity and perfection. They wish to surrender completely and become united and annihilated in their Beloved God.

Those people who seek the truth are so limited in number that in most cases could be ignorable. However, when they meet a true Master he shares all of his success and benefits with them, accepts them, surrenders his life, time, knowledge, experience and all achievements with them, coaches them up to the point where they become mature and wise enough that they will annihilate themselves in this Master and become one united devotee in all aspects and thus be able to continue their voyage by themselves. True Masters with full love and happiness inject their life into their disciples.

جمله معشوق است و عاشق پرده ای

In contrast the false masters amuse their poor followers who believe what they physically see; therefore they in their turn show their happiness and amusement with those outward shows of glory and glamour with glossy magazines, attractive music and quoting the sayings and poems from the teachings and life stories of the Masters in the past to their followers.

The true Master gradually, step-by-step takes his devoted disciple towards the sun, and while sheltering him from the beauty, heat, light and fire of the outside directs him into the core of the sun, where there is nothing but sun, all is sun and all is annihilation, in love devotion and meekness.

هر که جان خود را نتواند در راه دوست گذارد گو عاشقی را ترک نمای و از آن طریق قدم مگذار

Whoever is not capable to sacrifice his soul (Life) for the sake of his Beloved, advise him to abandon love and do not enter into that path.

Abu Ali Daghghaagh, Sufi master of the 4th Century AH from Nishapour

---

جمله معشوق است و عاشق پرده ای

DO NOT BREAK ANY HEART, AS EACH HEART

HAS A DIRECT CONNECTION TO GOD

One of the main goals of Sufism is to help, direct, and assist people to understand and to believe that the real happiness is not in luxury items, false images and ideas, wishes, fashionable goods, possessions and all of the other similar material many spend the whole of their life to locate, buy, obtain, and collect around themselves.

Happiness, tranquility, contentment, success, calmness and pleasure are qualities and a sense of feeling that is located inside the mind of people when and if they are prepared and ready to permit their heart to control and direct their mind. If a person lets the mind control his life and ignores his heart it will be disastrous.

Darvish-hood and Tasavvof—Sufism—teachings, advice and guidance for everyone is quite simple. It is extremely simple and uncomplicated. Darvish-hood wants and asks people to believe in the greatest fact and reality of life because when the fact is observed, considered and respected at the time of making a decision it will have great positive effects in all consequent situations that they will experience.

The fact is very simple:

Everyone is lovingly created by the same God, the only God, with the same love and equality in Creation, all have the same right and they are all equal to each other.

On this basis a fair and just person will never be misled by material desires and wants, it will be impossible for him to make any mistake; to damage anyone, to hurt anyone, to be unjust, unfair, dishonest, and cruel or have even one bad word for anyone, including themself. Of course, when a person does not damage others, they do not have to be worried, afraid of anything or anyone, and ashamed for his decisions or actions. In short the person will be HAPPY.

جمله معشوق است و عاشق پرده ای

One of major missions of this school is to help Mankind to understand, feel, believe and be convinced that the Khane ye Khooda—House of God—is located inside their own chest, in their own body. This house is the great repository of secrets; the secrets such as love, peace, happiness, fear, grief, sadness, pleasure and contentment. Their own heart is the most sacred holy, innocent temple. Man has to feel that it is the heart which is the highest holy ground, and on the same precious basis the same as the hearts of other people.

The mission and the duty of a Darvish, and the goal, target and intension of Darvish-hood and Sufism is to assist everyone to help themselves to feel the fact that God is not far away or out of reach, out of any contact, above in other planets and other worlds. The Loving, Glorious, Merciful, Beneficent, Creator God of the whole being is from eternity to eternity here with all, right now.

دل مســـوزان که ز هــر دل به خـــدا راهی هست. هر که را هیــچ به کــف نیســت

به دل آهـــی هست

Do not break a heart, as each heart has a direct connection to God

The person with no holdings may utter a sigh

Persian Poem

جمله معشوق است و عاشق پرده ای

SERVING, SERVING AND SERVING

This school's mission is to teach people to understand, feel and believe in their soul and heart, the principal fact that to reach God is very easy, the easiest task possible. Depending on their own intention and whether they are prepared and ready, they truly hope, intend and purify their feelings, thoughts and decisions in life; it is not difficult at all. It is simple to feel the presence of the Glorious Creator. Just look inside the heart and act accordingly.

For people to make themselves and/or another person truly and honestly peaceful and happy is to SERVE. Just serve no matter who, how, what, when or where. Serve anybody, anything and anyone but do it according to your full capacity and complete ability through LOVE and not only as a duty or desire for being recognised or praised.

The GOLDEN KEY to the temple of Love is to create happiness for other creatures sincerely and by true heartfelt SERVICE. The Temple of Love has no walls, gates, doors or windows it is all open from all sides.

The motto of a Darvish is *Serving, Serving and Serving*, serving by all of his ability and capacity, through all possible means and channels, a service with heartfelt love and devotion, without any show of expectation of reward, even not expecting the receiver of the service to know who did render the service or why.

The most sincere and purest devotion is to serve those who truly and honestly need the service, no matter in what level of society they may be or how they appear to be, e.g. among them may be bandits, rebels, and insurgents, people who have no stand in their society and are completely rejected. A Darvish knows that those people have already been judged and it is not up to the Darvish to judge them. The duty of the Darvish is to serve them. A Darvish must serve sincerely and through the heart. In reality those somehow unwanted people are the people who deserve

جمله معشوق است و عاشق پرده ای

more and need more sincere service and love, those are the people who are to be loved most and served best without any consideration of position or situation.

One word of love influences and works more productively and constructively than hundreds of years in punishment and imprisonment.

چشم بگشا که جلوه دلدار   متجلی است از در و دیوار

Open your eyes, manifestation of the Darling, Is manifesting from all around,

Persian Poem

A DARVISH IS A SLAVE OF LOVE AND

NOT A SERVANT OF REWARD

Another one of the principal ethics and foundational targets of the teachings and guidance of the path of Sufism is to teach, train and qualify the followers of the Path to purify both their main properties and qualities: inward as well as outward.

Darvish-hood or Sufism has set for itself a high and honourable obligation and goal. This mission is to assist and direct Darvishes to improve and elevate their internal, heartfelt feelings and develop wisdom which as the final consequence reflects outside the heart and mind conducting their actions. The way the Darvishes feel in heart, think and decide in mind and act in general.

The disciples first learn and practice the method to purify their inner qualities i.e. spirituality, asceticism, candid devotion and sincerity, and purify the conditions of their spirit (Soul)—Rooh from all dusty desires.

Based upon their capacity to learn, wayfarer Darvishes may need individual and personal counseling to adapt and determine the spiritual methods which will make it possible for them to arrive to the position of "a complete man", and be blessed with further advancements through their heartfelt services. This method of purification cooperates with and assists their soul to guide their thoughts, desires and instincts gradually, to become more and more purified and holy, in the direction of the teachings of The Path.

After this first step, the second step is to turn attention to the exterior quality of the disciples which may be explained as their manner, conduct, actions and the behaviour towards themselves, other people, animals, vegetation, inanimate or animate—the whole of Creation in general. The Darvish's deal with his own material existence—Jesm—as well as the way he thinks decides and acts.

جمله معشوق است و عاشق پرده ای

The exterior quality normally is a reflection and a consequence of the first, of the depth and connection to the heartfelt feelings and the correct and wise thoughts of the mind, if not in all but at least in most cases. Of course on some occasions the behaviour of people is conditioned, conditional and circumstantial.

The manners and behaviour of Man covers all of his actions starting from how he conducts himself privately, towards himself as an individual. From here it will be his social behaviour and physical actions in all aspects and dimensions i.e. his actions and behaviour towards other people, his social actions and activities, manners, conducts, as well as the services he provides to the society where he resides in.

In short, the teaching and training of Sufism directs all of the invisible qualities of the Darvish, the inner heartfelt feelings, thoughts and decisions. Consequently, such inner reflection and retreat improves the Darvish's actions and behaviour.

IT IS EASY TO CLAIM TO BE A DARVISH,

BUT HARD TO BE A TRUE ONE

Practically all people, Darvishes included, understand and agree that there are times and circumstances when a person's actions are out of his control. These actions may unconsciously be reactions to the actions of other people, the situation and/or time. The circumstances and conditions at the time of the occasion are mostly out of a person's control.

Many people accept unconscious reactions as normal. Those reactions are explained as reactions of living creatures against those actions out of their control which directly affect them. However even while enduring difficult occasions a Darvish is expected to be in full control of his thoughts, actions, and reactions and in general his nature, to govern properly over his consequent reactions and deeds. Sufis are to act according to the teachings, ethics, manners, and doctrine of the Maktab e Tasavvof and Darvish-hood. This school is the school of Love not reaction or revenge. The sincere devotee must consider the responsibilities of a meek, self—denied indigent and sincere wayfarer. The truthful Darvish must observe and contemplate with spiritual devotion all of his reflections and reactions towards or against other people and/or those circumstances governing the situation. During such harsh and difficult conditions the Darvish is strongly expected to happily accept, receive and absorb the hard blow of the situation as if he has been expecting the situation. It is easy to claim to be a Darvish, but hard to be a true one.

The teachings and training of the school are to assist, direct, and help the invited person to control, eliminate and correct his harsh reactions and replace them with his wise humble, pleasant and soft actions and/or reactions.

This Path assists devoted wayfarers to bear in their heart and mind that they have to face the consequences of their actions and conduct, as Hazrate Hagh has created them in love, as in fact and reality every creature is created in His love. Hagh's Godly

جمله معشوق است و عاشق پرده ای

love is bestowed on *all*, not a person or a group of persons. A Darvish learns not to forget his life is free and comes from Love and thus he spreads this light of love freely to his environment in all circumstances.

All human beings in particular and all creatures in general have His love free and we should give our love freely as a mirror reflects a ray of light shone upon it.

This part of the education and training is the most difficult part. This is the time the Darvish either surrenders to Hagh or, regretfully his Ego conquers his mind and he surrenders to Ego. The particular moment is when Darvish makes the conscious decision as Hazrate Hagh in His holy Book Qur'an says;

They are all free and they are all responsible.

The Maktab e Tasavvof—the school of Sufism and Darvish hood—helps the wayfarer to consider the final consequences of his decision and feel what will happen if he lets love control and direct his life or the consequences of going in the opposite direction and following egoistic desires and passions.

The devotee or disciple, to pass the heartfelt tests for him is to answer the following questions:

- ❖ Am I being humble and sincere?

- ❖ Am I being selfish and proud?

- ❖ Am I ready to serve?

- ❖ Am I wishing and expecting to be served?

All positive or negative, pleasant or unpleasant, proper and improper reflections of people are resultant from the decision made at this point. It is at this stage that the Darvish is expected to surrender to the Love of God and release the control of his instincts, desires, wishes, and passions. To lead his life the way Hagh wants him. Is he sincere, accepting, forgiving, honest, serving and, in short, loving or is he going astray?

مکتب درویشی و تصوف به دراویش می آموزد که پایگاه و سرزمین
جوانمردی و دلیری در دره ای قرار دارد که همانا دلهای انسان ها و آدمیان
است . سالکان ارادتمند و مومن را به این چنین سرزمین آبادانی راه هست .

اندر این سرزمین پر حلاوت بجز عشق چیزی را ارز و قیمتی نباشد.

نفرت , آزردن دیگران و کینه و بغض از جمله دشمنان و مخالفان عشق و
ارادتند و بدان جهت , در آن دنیای ملکوتی عشق و ارادت ایشان را پایگاهی
نیست. آن لکه های سیاه را در آسمان جبروت حضرت حق نشانی و ارزی
وجود ندارد. این بهشت صفا و سرزمین جلال و جبروت , مقام سالکان مخلص
است.

Sufism assists Darvishes to feel that the land of chivalry and

generosity is located in the valley of the heart of other

people wherein the pious and devoted are worthy to enter.

In this valley nothing is of any value or glory but love.

Hatred, spite and rancour are the enemies and oppositions

to the love and devotion therefore they possess no position

in this kingdom of Lord HAGH-- The Truth. The belief of

the devotees resides here in this land of glory.

Abbas Ali Shah, One of the Masters of the Path

A DARVISH IS TO BE THE COTTON WOOL, NOT ROCK.

A person who has registered himself in this school of meekness and sincerity, but has an ego which does not surrender, and is not prepared to accept, receive and absorb any hard, unpleasant actions or misbehaviour of other people towards him, must review and study his thoughts very carefully. A Darvish who is not prepared to bear the behaviour of other people that he considers harsh, unfair, unjust and wrong, or if such person is not ready to accept happily the difficult situations or unpleasant environment, this person is advised that he must REPENT. This person should start the Path from start, and scold his ego.

For those people who are unable and are not ready to accept what they receive as it happens and in return treat others with pure and sincere love and devotion it is better for them to repent, and start their spiritual practices from the very beginning but this time with more seriousness and sincere determination and hope than before.

A Darvish must always remember that the consequences and results for his unwise reaction to other people's action (no matter if he considers those actions fair or unfair or even misbehavior by other people), will be for the most part harder and more painful than the harsh action he has already received from those people.

For example, supposing a heavily weighted rock falls from a height of one hundred metres onto another hard rock. What will happen? The answer is easy and simple they both will be crushed. Of course the one which is less strong will break and be damaged more.

Now let us assume the same heavily weighted rock falls from the same height on same weight of material but not rock this time, let's say that it falls onto cotton wool. What will happen now? Of course the answer again is simple and easy. The cotton wool will not be damaged or affected much and the rock will not be affected either and/or if a damage occurred it will be ignorable and insignificant.

The above example represents the physical, psychological and spiritual effect of an unexpected behaviour (even bad luck or accident) or action by a person towards another.

A Darvish is to be the cotton wool, not rock.

A Darvish is to bear the hardship and not be the cause of the hard ship.

As per the teaching and the training of Sufism, a Darvish learns and prepares to behave in all of his actions and reactions the way The Most Beloved Hagh wants him to i.e. to adore Creation, admire Creation, love Creation and be so immersed in the love for and of Creation, that he sees everyone or everything as another pure example of the love of the Great Creator and His Creation. Through such devotion the Darvish learns that he is never to complain about whatever he faces, but on the contrary, accepts all with gratefulness and thanks.

جمله معشوق است و عاشق پرده ای

A COMPLETE MAN

To a Darvish the whole of Creation is Love. A Darvish believes that the Creation from eternity to eternity has come in to existence and was created by Hagh by virtue of His love. Life is love, people are love, and living or not living creatures are love. Therefore his motto is

LOVE, LOVE and LOVE

Love is truthfully and sincerely the only reality. A Darvish must believe in this, the greatest fact of Creation, the Darvish is expected to show his belief in practical action truly and not just in hollow, empty, dry and tasteless words. Sufism or Darvish-hood is true heartfelt actions and not simple colourful words.

> عشق دامی است که حضرت حق فرا راه ارادتمندان خویش مقرر فرموده
>
> *LOVE is the trap installed by Hagh –*
>
> *The Trap in the way of devoted person.*
>
> Abu Saeed

A Darvish is to show love in his daily action and behaviour, in offering, in his giving, receiving, accepting and granting. A Darvish must render true service by surrendering to Love. He must not just use the tongue in saying the word L O V E which if not shown in action is only an empty, useless, improper and cheap word. A Darvish is to show L O V E truly in practice and in action.

جمله معشوق است و عاشق پرده ای

A truly devoted Darvish is a person who is well prepared to sacrifice his jugular vein to create heartfelt happiness and satisfaction to any creature who needs his help, assistance, cooperation and his love.

Recently I witnessed the following: A man was on the telephone talking to a Darvish in another city, over one thousand kilometres away. Although they had not met in person they spoke once a week and he was discussing with her (the Darvish) his family concerns. His wife has heart problems and had recently been to see an eye specialist regarding an eye problem and was told there was no hope to save her eyes. The Darvish, upon hearing this says "Ask your specialist when he would like me to be there and I will donate my eye to your lady." The Darvish, who herself suffers health problems, did not ask whether the eye was needed, whether or not the specialist had suggested he could do this surgery or whether the man and his wife had even considered this possibility. She just said she would give her eye to a person who needed it.

A Body is not eternal, it perishes; while love and all good deeds out of love are eternal, will stay on and live on forever.

Sufism first directs, teaches and assists Sufis or Darvishes to elevate, improve, purify and govern, control and direct, train and guide their thoughts and their consequent actions.

Secondly it teaches the Darvishes how they can create a sincere, pure and wise way of life, correct behaviour for their instincts and desires, sincerity for their spirituality, and to control their physical ordinary day to day life.

The Darvishes progress to higher levels of spirituality when they sincerely practice what the Maktab e Tasavvof offers and teaches them. This improvement and advancement greatly depends upon their own sincerity, belief, agreement and feelings of heartfelt affection and love towards becoming a better citizen of this world and of course improving their Seyr (spiritual travel and voyages or advancement) which is their highest goal and target to be blessed and become "A Complete Man".

Darvishes will succeed in cleansing their mind by gradually training the mind and thoughts in the direction their master or teacher directs them, which in turn improves their actions and reactions gradually and simultaneously. By following the spiritual

جمله معشوق است و عاشق پرده ای

teachings and guidance of their teacher, and above all by the blessing of the Most Beloved Hagh, they will develop the condition of their heart. To achieve this high goal and hoped for consequent advantages Darvishes have to work hard in the same way a person who wishes to be successful in any material field, subject and/ or any profession in this life must.

As Man hopes and endeavours to cleanse his mind and perform right actions, The Most Beloved Allah bestows blessings of purification upon his heart.

It is evident that in this world nothing either materially, spiritually or heartfelt will be achieved unless we sacrifice all transient worldly pleasures which are in a different way than our heartfelt goal and try our best towards the direction we have set our hopes upon. In the spiritual and holy path of life not only is it vital, but surely, surely very hard to start. Ascending to higher stations and positions of spirituality requires belief, hope, sincerity, determination, practice, sacrifice, endeavour and of course proper guidance by a true teacher. All of these, when sincere, receive the blessing of the Most Beloved Allah, The Great Creator.

The first foundational step on the Path of Truth is to die; that is, to come out of the awareness of Self, being slave of passions and desires of (I), and become reborn as the slave of the Absolute Truth and Reality.

On the path Darvishes and Sufis travel there are numerous Roohaani (Spiritual) and Jesmaani (Physical) conditions which they may pass through and can be described as crossing deserts of temptations, uncertainties and tests, fields of progress, mountains of difficulties and sadness, storms of grief, as well as the farms of happiness.

For a Darvish passing through all of those levels, crossing all of those plains, deserts, fields, climbing those mountains and enjoying those farms there may come the time when he arrives to the position of being prepared to become A COMPLETE MAN.

For a Darvish to reach the station that his heart hopes for, lots of spiritual as well as physical and material preparations based on discipline and mortification are required. The first step, which is not an easy one at all, is discovering *how* to find and to practice the best way and the method most suitable to the person's condition and locating the proper method to help him most effectively in order to tame, control and eliminate wishes and expectations of his ego, self—centering, passion, desire and material existence. A Peer, Morshed, Master or Teacher is the person who is capable to direct and help the Wayfarer.

To overcome the egotism and selfish desires will be an extremely difficult task, most definitely. This goal will be achieved only after the person learns the method and practice that will assist him in the controlling of passions, improper worldly and materialistic desires and demands.

This method when properly practiced according to the teaching and guidance of a Master or Peer will improve the condition of the mind of the wayfarer towards the right and proper direction and to direct the mind to act under heart's command. This is not an easy task and should start with devotion, honestly and sincerely practicing service to all of the creatures of the world, and through love and affection create and sacrifice material comfort. The Darvish, to achieve such a high goal, is expected to do his best in offering his sincere services to others. His intention for each one of his thoughts, actions and attempts must be pure and sincere, which surely renders positive and creative results and helps him to achieve positive results from his devotion. This step, the vital step on the PATH is:

SINCERITY, SINCERITY, SINCERITY AND SINCERITY

To be a Darvish does not mean to be registered in a Selseleh it is to practice devotion, service, to serve and sincerely serve. There have been, there are and there will be women and men who lived all of their life as a true devotee and not only no-one knows, but even they may never know that fact themselves.

Please do not forget this fact that; anyone who registers his name in the Maktab e Tasavvof but fails to practice at least the above points, and does not take serious steps in purifying his life is at least a failure if not a liar, and a pretender.

جمله معشوق است و عاشق پرده ای

A SINCERE DARVISH FLIES ON THE WINGS OF HAGH

While a Darvish constantly and sincerely continues all of that which has been ordered and recommended by his Master and his Sheykh he will accordingly continually and gradually progress and improve. Such spiritual and heartfelt improvement corresponds to his endeavour as well as to his capacity. It must be reminded that although in this spiritual path the Darvish's intention and endeavour has value the, main power behind every success is from the Beloved Hagh. A sincere Darvish on this holy Path flies on the wings of Hagh. The Darvish is only the navigator of his own instincts, for example as a child is carried in the arms of his mother, she is carrying him to wherever she will, but the child thinks it is he who has made it alone.

The time will come that the Darvish becomes powerful and able enough to properly direct his materialistic wishes and control his egotism and will surrender to love and devotion. From this point the DARVISH WILL NOT EXIST ANY MORE. Physically he does; he breathes, he eats, he sleeps, he drinks, he talks, he walks, he works and he performs his human social and family duties with heartfelt love. Ego, passions, anger, greed and grief as well as any other habit or ugly evil nature loses its' grip upon this devotee, and has no more control over him. This Darvish does not obey or follow his material desires, self—centering, greed, anger, jealousy and passions. Whatever he does is according to the commands of LOVE. Love directs him, and from then on he will want whatever his heart wants him to want. With this constant connection he happily continues devotedly and quite sincerely in his life practicing what the Sheykh teaches and following where he leads him to. This complete obedience and sincere practicing elevates his spiritual condition which consequently expands the scope of his moralities, improves his social manners and helps him to be meek and modest person (Seyr and consequent Solook).

When a person sincerely understands and feels that he is nothing but a mirror receiving rays of love and light radiating on him from Hagh, such a person does in his turn reflect those rays of love and light to the whole world properly and completely to the best of his capacity. When a Darvish is so sincere and does his

جمله معشوق است و عاشق پرده ای

duty as properly as he can it will be the time that the Darvish starts to travel deeper and deeper into his spiritual world.

The Darvish, through his heart, will note that true life is in loving to help and to serve, so, this Darvish finds that without sincere meekness and indigence he and/ or any other person in a position such as him is nothing but a dark, lifeless piece of material unable to perform anything. This condition is an important feeling, the feeling an ordinary, materialistic person has no comprehension or understanding for at all. When the Darvish reaches this high point of wisdom it is the beginning of the time where he has started walking on the Path of the Truth.

The Darvish is at the stage of meekness and self-denial, which is the centre point for giving advantage to other people's rights over his own. This person is at the head of the road of Darvish-hood, embodying Sufism—indigent and poor. From this moment onward he owns and has nothing for himself but in fact does not want and does not claim anything for himself. Such a person is so shiny and bright in his society; people who are in contact with him feel the light and warmth of that purity and sincerity in him. Those people feel, see, recognize and benefit from his LOVE, the love extended to all of them, they see in him nothing but light and happiness, giving and serving.

This is a true and real position achieved or better to say arrived at, by his devotion. Since he has purified and cleansed his heart, mind, thoughts and actions so sincerely, rays of Hagh's blessings and Love shines through him to his environment.

While claiming to be a Darvish is easy, arriving truly at the station of FAGHR (meek and indigence) is not easy. On the contrary is a very difficult wish to attain, still gladly possible.

All Monotheists believe in Hagh the One True God. Beyond this, a Darvish erases whatever is not Hagh from the temple of love, his heart. The God a Darvish worships is the Creator of existence, Absolute Love, Absolute Being, The Only One God, of Kindness, Grace, purity and Love. The Great Architect of the world.

According to Darvishes belief how could Great Lord God of such grace and generosity, granting love, giving, mercy and favour act out of anger, revenge, punishment, torture, fire, and rage? Heyhaat, Heyhaat. IMPOSSIBLE, IMPOSSIBLE.

جمله معشوق است و عاشق پرده ای

Jesus Christ the Prophet of God says:

GOD IS LOVE.

Also according to Darvish belief, Allah, the One who creates, bestows life, knows all secrets, and is aware of and grants all needs, what good to Him are His creatures supplications, mortifications, fervor, strivings, asceticism, piety and virtue?

Any such teaching given to human beings is for their own benefit, the spiritual health and tranquility of soul. To give, to forgive and to be charitable, Allah Almighty wants His created Man serve his fellow.

A Darvish, submerged in the love of the Most Beloved, contemplates and commemorates Hagh by and through his whole existence—a sincere soul, heart and spirit, mind, thoughts and wisdom together with vigilance and remembrance of God. Based on that holiness the Darvish lovingly serves and humbly helps all Creation, whether plants or animals, and all of humankind white or yellow, black or red, wealthy or poor, friend or stranger since they all are rays from Everlasting Light of Hagh. This sincerity, free from hypocrisy and dissimulation, known as Solook and spiritual advancement of the heart known as Darvish's Seyr are the two wings assisting him to ascend towards his Beloved Hagh's Absolute Being.

An Arab asked Hazrate Ali: "Do you see Allah?"

Hazrate Ali answered, "I do not worship whom I do not SEE."

Remember Hagh in private. Sincere service to His creatures gradually eliminates the egoistic pride of the Darvish and cleanses him or her. Love for the Beloved in the heart and humble service to His people, purifies and transforms darkness and impurities in the Darvish. Thus he beholds and enjoys the everlasting light of HAGH in all. On this day he sees all truthfulness and facts of life as did Hazrate Ali.

THE MAN OF TRUTH, LOVE AND DEVOTION

Darvish-hood or Sufism is the school founded and established for training, preparing, assisting and helping the devoted Darvish to reach to such a stage of purity that the rays of Hagh's blessings and love shines through him. The school is fully prepared and fully responsible to direct the Darvish and to prepare and make him realise and discover capacities vested in him. In this Maktab, the disciple finds the right way to prepare, practice, offer and render his power, ability, capacity; and beyond that to serve love and to obey the governance of love and devotion over his instincts and passion in all respects.

Once this meek and indigent person is so clean and pure that the rays of the true love of Hazrate Hagh are observable through his actions and reactions, no matter what Sufi or Darvish position, condition and/or social level, no matter if he possesses either the highest position or the simplest, if he is the most well-known man in his society or not, in reality he is the man of Truth, love and devotion. People see not him or his position, his wealth or situation but they observe the light that they feel in their society, the warmth of his LOVE. They see the condition of his heart.

All of the attentions and endeavours of this devoted person are concentrated on his duty, providing truthfulness, honesty and positive intention, and performing whatever help and service possible, with heartfelt affection.

A true and sincerely devoted Darvish is, while he is travelling on the Path of Truth, similar to a school student who day by day gathers more knowledge and adds to his education, gradually progressing and improving his Rooh (soul) va Jesm (body). This devoted person gradually enters the ocean of love, where he has the opportunity to further purify his heart and soul. The further he submerses in that great ocean, the more heartfelt love and service he provides. This process continues over and over until the time where his being is fully submersed in love and bringing faultless and perfect results into his environment, which of course will have reflection on his life as well.

جمله معشوق است و عاشق پرده ای

When the actions of the Darvish display an honest cooperation with the Master and his actions are blessed by the coaching and heartfelt grace of his Master both the Master and the Devotee will have the blessing of Hagh. The blessing is in favour of their proper actions, and blossoms with glory and beauty. This will appear and shine brighter in their hearts which then flows out into their environment, to everyone, every minute and every second.

This position and place is not an ordinary or simple one, it is not what everyone can achieve without serious sincerity and purity, intention, attempt, hope, wish and hard work. After a person or disciple completely surrenders and dies out of his egoistic, worldly desires, wishes and demands; and when this meek person proves he does not exist, the blessing of the Beloved brightens him, takes him out of himself, blesses him and makes him a Godly person. The devotee from this position governs his spiritual and material life and brings them under his control, obedience and command, so that both of his senses and desires behave themselves properly and in accordance with love, dignity, honesty and affection for purity and service towards all creatures.

No one may enter this place and receive this position unless being completely burned in the Fire of Love, the ashes of his egoistic desires and wants to be scattered by the winds of self—denial and self-sacrifice on the fields of service.

This of course seems to be the most difficult intention, work, and mission but is possible and the results achieved from this blessed and holy condition will be glorious, so great that it cannot easily be imagined. To an ordinary and materially thinking person this condition is unbelievable.

GIVING IS MORE BLESSED THAN RECEIVING

Sufism directs and coaches the Darvish to improve in all directions and aspects of life. The Maktab trains the Darvish to feel that one of the most important targets for a Darvish should be to serve. Sufism teaches, directs and guides the Darvish to act lovingly, morally and ethically in all aspect of his life, particularly while dealing with other creatures. The Darvish in each case, whether in vital matters of life or not, has to respond using his properly prepared conduct and focus in the direction bound to qualities expected from a Darvish (i.e. a meek person with no personal greed). A truly sincere, well trained, well educated, wise and sincere Sufi is a servant of Creation, a devotee to serve to the maximum of his capacity, rendering service freely without expectation to whomever and/or whatever requires service and help. Colour, religion, nationality, gender, marital status, education and/or position of the person receiving that service are not of his concern.

The Maktab trains Darvishes to practice giving love and devotion no matter how hard it appears to be at the beginning. This practice helps the Darvish to love and serve his society irrespective of the size, irrespective of whether they are immediate family, the next-door neighbour, people from the next street, other village, town or city, citizens of other countries. At the time service is required the Darvish is blind, blind to any secondary matter, what the Darvish sees is the service required, and his own duty to provide service.

This pure love not only produces positively constructive and purifying results for the Darvish but also extends to other people automatically. Positive results gained from good deeds and proper actions brings happiness and contentment to all involved; starting from the Darvish initially, then extended outward towards other people around him and then from there to those who reside in his society. Heartfelt happiness will be with the Darvish as long as the life giving rays of sincere love and service pours out of his heart freely towards other creatures.

جمله معشوق است و عاشق پرده ای

Whoever is blessed by the great gift and honour of loving other people and serving them, whoever extends warm and shining rays of love to others, is the one who receives the blessing, happiness, glory and purity prior to those who receive them.

Jesus Christ said: *Giving is more blessed than receiving.*

A Darvish is to serve his society purely, devotedly, sincerely and innocently irrespective if that society agrees with him or not, likes him or not, respects him or not.

A Darvish is to SERVE, according to the command of his heart and not to judge, comment or follow the decision of his ego, desires, passion, judgment, selfishness or any other decision made on such an unclean basis.

The only person that a Sufi or Darvish is obliged to seriously judge and comment upon, and not to have any kindness, forgiveness or ignoring of even the smallest venial fault of that person is himself, and no one else.

گفت آتش بی سبب بی نفروختم

Fire replied, I did not blaze for no cause

دعوی بی معنیت را سوختم

but to burn out your reasonless claims

Moulana Rumi

THE DEEPER THE FARMER CUTS THE HEART OF EARTH, THE BETTER THE CROP WILL GROW.

The role and duty of a Master as the principal of the Maktab in the life of a Darvish is to advise, teach, train and assist him to follow the feelings of his sincere heart. Success will be achieved through sincere and honest cooperation between disciple and his Sheykh; the teacher being an experienced, wise, humble and kind leader correcting and eliminating imperfection in His disciple. The Sheykh will direct the disciple to open the scope of his vision, in order to evaluate his mind's decisions, proper or improper actions and behaviour towards himself and towards other people

For the Darvish the vital goal of purification is achieved with the guidance and assistance of the Peer, Master, or Master's Sheykh in finding and locating his faults, his dark points, each improper thought, action, and behaviour. It is the first step and the starting point for travel towards true spiritual happiness.

Thus the disciple through the guidance of his Sheykh will eliminate whatever is wrong in his thoughts, ideas and even dreams. Thus in the Maktab, a Master:

❖ Firstly trains, guides and helps the Darvish to open his heart to love for Hazrate Hagh and His Creatures, and that anything else consequently is a blessing from Hagh.

❖ Assists, guides and helps to search deep inside the Darvish's mind sincerely and wisely so that the Darvish can discover his own faults

❖ Assists guides and helps the Darvish to understand that by conducting his life and actions according to the teachings and guidance of the order he will correct his improper thoughts, wishes and desires.

جمله معشوق است و عاشق پرده ای

❖ Trains, guides and helps the Darvish, with the belief that the Blessing of Allah, the Almighty and Most Merciful, will be directing his thoughts, intentions and practices to lovingly and sincerely serve.

To help the Darvish identify his imperfections, correct them and eliminate them, is not an easy process. It is not achieved in one lesson or by using teachings of limited consequences and effects but by locating and cleansing the main causes inside his mind, causes which are creating improper and wrong physical actions of any kind and nature.

It is within the mind that the influence of egoistic desires and passions create faults that are grown and promoted then through bodily actions exist. Self-centering, pride and boastful behaviour is a desire from loose and uncontrolled instincts, looking down at people is the fruit of selfishness, cheating is a consequence of greed, aggression from an inferior and fearful mind, and all of them are from a poor and unclean heart.

It is necessary to advise that it is the teacher's sincerity, devotion, honesty, ascetism, sentiment, meekness and indigence that is the most important and vital quality to conduct a disciple towards absolute truth. A shaky, materialistic, selfish, egoistical person is an improper person and he himself needs a guide and director to save him from himself, he is not fit to conduct the role of a guide.

After a Darvish discovers his faults he sincerely tries to cleanse them. This cleansing process is the solid foundation for eliminating the wrong and unholy products of his mind and its thoughts i.e. his success will show an immediate and direct reflection upon his actions and behaviours.

As a consequence of this purification and cleansing a Darvish controls his egoistic desires, wishes and actions and behaves towards everybody with love, sincerity and honesty. A Darvish at this point of purity behaves with pure affection, sincerity and love towards all creatures; he accepts, welcomes and greets them with a smiling face and serves them with love. The Darvish does not permit or allow himself to judge other people.

If a Darvish receives something unpleasant and unexpected, the Darvish, in order to find the main cause and reason for such punishment, must examine and research his own thoughts and actions.

Darvish and Sufi must judge their own manners and not the reaction from the outside.

A Darvish must be lovingly thankful for the right actions of people towards each other and forgive what he sees as their wrong deeds or actions and/or their possible misbehaviour towards him. Such a devoted Darvish in exchange for either people's love and devotion, or unpleasant or improper actions, renders his service lovingly. He who is travelling towards Absolute Truth reacts and responds by giving his pure love similar to a spring which pours out fresh and clean water out of its heart to whoever who is thirsty.

One of the best examples and symbols of purity and holiness to a Darvish is Jesus. After his enemies slandered, whipped and did to him the most miserable actions they were able to do, in exchange for all of those tortures Jesus asked God the Most Glorious, Forgiving, Beneficent and Merciful to forgive them. On the Cross, Jesus asked his Beloved Darling Creator:

"O' Father forgive these people as they do not know what they are doing"

Another example for love and devotion is Hosain e Mansoor e Hallaj. During his time the fanatical people of Baghdad did not understand his heartfelt motives and words, did not understand what he was telling them and directing them towards. Those people, because of their lack of proper knowledge and/or jealous, fanatical, thoughts imprisoned him for 11 years before they decided to torture him by chopping

جمله معشوق است و عاشق پرده ای

off his hands and legs. Not satisfied with this they then hanged him, decapitated him, cut and chopped his body into pieces and burned them in fire. This did not even placate them, deciding finally to spread his ashes into the waves of the sea. But in spite of all of that, while those fanatics were doing all of those harsh tortures to him, Hosain e Mansoor e Hallaj was smiling joyfully to them and asking his Darling Beloved God to pardon them and forgive their actions as, according to him, their actions were out of their ignorance and not due to proper wisdom and/ or knowledge.

Jesus is a leading Darvish

Hallaj is a true Darvish.

And similar things have happened more or less to considerably large numbers of the other innocent and true servants of Humanity, their love unappreciated, those sincere lovers of Hagh accused of all sorts of things, up to the point where they sacrificed their material life for their faith. They were killed but in reality those innocent people were still alive, are alive and will be alive forever and ever.

Earth receives all the rubbish, garbage and harsh action of the people and in return gives them all necessities they need to live; water, food, shelter and all the tools to support their lives.

A Sufi or Darvish should mould his behaviour and reactions towards other people from the example of Earth; live, serve like and think as being Earth:

Darvishes believe that the real and true or complete existence and being of Man is not limited only to their ordinary material or physical life. The true and effective life of Man consists of the life of both their heart, and then their well looked after, well managed and well controlled mind; which in its turn controls their material or physical being, actions and behaviour.

It is the bright reflection from the proper cooperation of heart and the mind, the two different components, which produces the real character of a person, loving or vice versa.

TRUE MEMBERS OF THE FAMILY

A Darvish is to devote and dedicate his complete existence to serving everyone and everything. His service is to be offered without any question or reasoning. A Darvish must believe that anything he offers or any action that he does that is not founded on this pure and holy foundation, or lacks sincerity, that the action is not truly for the sake of Hagh; it is an act of charity. It is only to satisfy his own ego and therefore such an action, no matter of what nature, quality or quantity, has no spiritual value and therefore the person must not consider himself a disciple in the path of Hagh—The Absolute Truth. Anybody who wishes recognition for his services is not a devotee but a labourer who works for wages.

People who hope for rewards or prizes in exchange for their "good deeds" must understand that their action would be exactly the same as the work of a labourer who works because he at the end of the day expects to receive a proper wage for his labour. What else should a labourer expect? He does not deserve anything more than his wage. He wanted a wage and he received a wage. Whereas the sons and daughters of a family who have a family business accomplish all work required, whether it is easy or hard; but why? Because it is their own home, their own family, their own reputation. They do not expect any wage or salary or prize or anything of the kind.

Being the Creation of Beloved Hagh, by his love, are we not all children, owners of the same home, and true members of the same family? What else can be of any value or importance?

All of the acts of benevolence by Darvishes must be sourced from pure love and based on devotion; donations and dedications, giving and helping and/or good deeds performed or rendered by any person, no matter if he is or is not recognised by his society as a Darvish, has to have its roots deep in LOVE. This giving person should sincerely believe that without honest heartfelt faith whatever has been done or given has no value.

جمله معشوق است و عاشق پرده ای

A Darvish is to serve all people without laying down any condition or distinction as to who or what deserves. A Darvish is a meek person who is to help others without any reserve, without expectation. Darvish accepts all hardship with an open, happy and smiling face. A Darvish does not desire or hope for the return of any favour. Anybody who has this kind of material and earthly desire is wrongfully wearing the garb of pure and innocent people.

A true Darvish does not serve other people or creatures because he expects God to grant him a huge and beautiful palace in His paradise in heaven, a palace built from bricks of gold and silver. To the Darvish His love is the true and real paradise, the happiness of the person receiving his service is His glorious palace. The key to Paradise is the happy and satisfied smile of the receiver of his service.

O BELOVED, CURE COMES FOR YOUR

TIRED WOUNDS AND PAIN

A Darvish believes that the most Glorious Darling, Hagh, observes his thoughts, desires, actions and works of all quality and nature. He believes Hagh expects devotees' complete love to be rendered to all of Hagh's Creation therefore he does everything to prove his fidelity, sincerity, devotion, affection, service, help and assistance, as well as to prove himself worthy enough for Hagh's expectation. A true Darvish is a simple independent mature and determined person who has surrendered his life completely to service the whole of Creation.

By enrolling and registering in this Maktab, the disciple promises to himself and undertakes in his heart to follow and practice the proper method of devotion and service to the others according to the needs of the needy. He is also determined to choose the best possible way to devote his life to the complete service of everybody and everything that requires and needs service. Based upon this holy Oath, this sacred foundation, he lovingly chooses the best way for service and on such a pure and proper base his life will be pleasant, happy and he will enjoy his devotion.

چون شفا ای دلربا از خستگی و درد تو است

O beloved, cure comes for your tired
wounds and pain,

خسته را مرهم مساز و درد را درمان مکن

Don't apply ointment to pain

Persian Poem

جمله معشوق است و عاشق پرده ای

It is not easy to ascend to higher spiritual stations unless the person is truly sincere and wishing to endeavour by all power and ability. The Darvish will face enormous spiritual, emotional, mental and material challenges. The traveler sometimes faces very difficult periods and the next moment, everything appears to be easy and soft to pass through. One trial may seem to last for a very long and endless time and another may appear to pass as fast as lightning in the sky. Duration, type, nature, appearance and all other qualities and conditions of those occasions and times cannot be known to anyone and are never the same for two different persons, as each person goes at his own pace on his own Path.

The only advice for anyone who gets annoyed, tired, cooled down, depressed, angry, or loses hope and love for advancement is that: with that kind of thinking they will never get anywhere and unless they cast all of their heart on their true path of love and go against this sort of cheating of their mind they will hopelessly remain wherever they are. The hard times, the difficult road, the hotter sun and greater thirst do not make the wayfarer despair and disappointed but on the contrary they make the true devotee more and more eager and thirsty to keep steadfast and continue on the Path.

Darvish-hood requires, expects and guides Darvishes to be cautious and to be alert against their own devil (desires, expectations, wishes, egoistic passions and self-centering). Sufism helps the Darvish to succeed in cleansing his inside and cleaning his exterior conditions and qualities accordingly.

مال و زر و چیز رایگان باید باخت

Wealth, gold and possessions should give free,

چون کار به جان رسید جان باید باخت

when the time tightens for life, should give life.

Persian Poem

The Blessing of Hazrate Hagh, the sincerity and devotion of the Darvish, the close obedience of devotee to Master and his Sheykh's teachings, directions, assistance, help and guidance, are the wayfarer's capital and luggage on this spiritual voyage.

A Darvish does not observe Creation as a mere transient and mortal system, he believes in higher causes and reason beyond Creation. In his heart he entirely values that gracious reason and adjusts his life according to that high, glorious and precious rule. All Darvishes have to obey and follow this heartfelt feeling without questioning or expectation since that is commanded by Hagh:

Serve and do not expect reward.

Serve and do not wish to be served.

The Sheykh's blessing is the first powerful action of help for the Darvish. Sheykh and Darvish together lovingly work, study, experience, suffer, enjoy and progress, advance and improve. This important relationship is the foundation of Darvish-hood. A Darvish sincerely and obediently follows the teachings and the direction the Master conducts him in. A Darvish believes that his Master elevates him from his ordinary and low conditions, coaches him to travel upwards until the time he elevates to the highest condition possible for him, the time hopefully by blessing of Hazrate Allah, he becomes A COMPLETE MAN.

> *Piety in private,*
>
> *donating charity at the time of need,*
>
> *patience when misfortunes come,*
>
> *toleration at the time of anger,*
>
> *truthfulness when there is fear,*
>
> *are qualities A Complete Man enjoys.*
>
> Iman Zainul Abedin, the great grandson of
> Prophet Mohammad

جمله معشوق است و عاشق پرده ای

To be A COMPLETE MAN is different from material measures people have in mind, such a person is far beyond the external appearances. A Complete Man is in his heart and mind different from the ordinary person, and his feelings, views, thoughts and wishes, values and his wisdom are all founded on different qualities from the type of person who thinks materialistically. The Complete Man's thinking is completely different from the materialist. His observation, thinking, decisions and the way of acting are far above and beyond what can be described because his spiritual station, position and condition as well as his decision making mind are located and based in absolute obedience to his Heart. The life of such a devoted person is mixed with much higher love and feeling for the whole of Creation. A Complete Man is different, a holy man, and quite apart from those who see the world as only a materially existing transient life.

The true values of real life are inside a Darvish, values bestowed inside the heart, not outside him. By his honest heart and the mind making right decisions and his consequent proper and right actions people easily observe and see that negative thoughts, and improper action and reactions have no grip and power on such COMPLETE MAN at all.

A Darvish may or may not hold a high social position, may be rich or poor, educated or ordinary, handsome or ugly. A Darvish is quiet, kind, serving, loving and forgiving, he is humble, indigent, devoted, affectionate and loving in action. A sincere Darvish is meek, honest, quiet and with a deep heart; deeper in love than any of the oceans. He does not expect any recognition for his service, and he lovingly ignores other people's annoyance and/or any possible harm they may do to him; he does not see and/or deem anything to be ugly and bad. To him, from this high heartfelt position, whatever a Darvish sees is beautiful and glamorous since he sees through the eyes of his darling Hagh. Who is a Darvish to see or think anything but Love? Hagh creates from His Love; He gives and bestows nothing but Love to all. A Darvish is one of the "all".

Anyone who thinks talks and acts as and according to the above qualities is honoured to be a true and real human—A COMPLETE MAN—in reality and in nature.

In five different places in the holy Qur'an Our Lord God or Allah says: We created Man from dust or soil (In one place Allah says from BLACK Soil) and blew in him from Our Soul.

جمله معشوق است و عاشق پرده ای

This fact clarifies two important points to Man.

First, all human beings are images of our Lord, God; we all are created as children of God, pure, blessed, constructive, creative and holy. He is pure and spiritual, loves, adores, admires and respects.

Second, all Mankind is created from material soil or dust, in other words we are created in the material world. Hence we think materially, want the best of material advantages for our comfort, leisure, pleasure, happy and pleasant times. Man wants to put in less effort and achieve the highest possible results.

God has created Man in His own image but what does this mean? What message does this convey to Mankind? What benefit does it have? And what duties does the man have in return?

Over those two qualities granted to Man, he is created free to make decisions. This means Man is free to make his decisions based on his material interests or completely spiritual, and/or in between and logically in combination of both of those two qualities to his capacity.

Man's brain or mind is the protector of his material part, and his heart is the temple of love and devotion.

If the mind is left alone and uncontrolled it will go astray and thus the mind is the DEVIL of the man, because it takes him down towards his material desires. When the enemy is inside the house the struggle is harder and more difficult.

جمله معشوق است و عاشق پرده ای

اگر آدمی به چشم است و دهان و گوش و بینی

If humanity is to be considered by the eyes and
mouth, ear and nose

چه میان نقش دیوار و میان آدمیت

Then what difference is there

between a picture on the wall or a man

به حقیقت آدمی باش و گر نه دیو باشی

Indeed be a true man or you are a demon

که فرشته ره ندلرد به مقام آدمیت

Even angels cannot admit to the station of true man.

A Persian mystic poem

IT IS EASY TO BE JUST A JUDGE, BUT TERRIBLY
HARD TO BE A JUST JUDGE

قضاوت ساده است اما عدالت مشگل است

It is easy to be a judge,

but terribly hard to be a just judge

Hazrate Ghadeer Ali Shah

Currently lectures, teachings and discussions about ethics, morals, manners and the good behaviour of people towards each other (which is the second quality bestowed on Man) has been receiving special attention.

Gladly there are numerous religious societies, legal policies, social organizations, clubs, and associations established with the intention to teach, train and guide people to reform and improve their way of thinking and their behaviour towards others. The goal being that they will uphold their ethics, morality and observe proper behaviour particularly when dealing with other people. Those organizations teach their policy and their preferred behaviour method to the people, advising them to observe expectations of sincerity, sharing, honesty, compassion and charity on the basis of purity.

Religions, in exchange for the followers religious attributes, ethics, proper and good deeds, promise eternal glory and high rewards. On the contrary, for misbehaviour and ignoring the commands and laws of religion, they promise eternal punishments and hardship in the next coming world. The social societies, legislation, and organizations in their turn have prepared, issued and invented imprisonments,

جمله معشوق است و عاشق پرده ای

loss of social rights, financial penalties and punishments for those who ignore their social duties or ignore laws and regulations imposed.

Some societies have been successful to achieve their goals and make their members and followers obedient to their laws and rules. Some others are continuing to improve and achieve themselves a place in moral society. A number of other societies are still struggling to persuade their followers and audiences to understand and accept their message. In any case, their attempts have to be admired and respected since they are doing their part in the elimination of wrong actions. It should be admitted that all of those systems and/or organizations are trying hard and doing their best to improve the manners and behaviour of their members and people in private and in society.

In other words, every one of the above organizations according to their laws, rules, constitution, position, condition, capacity and ability are doing something positive to improve the manners of their people and correct and amend the weak points in their morals, manners and behaviour and actions either in their society or towards each other in private. Those organizations try and work hard toward the improvement of their society within the scope of their constitution and policy.

Those societies do everything they can to create a safe, successful and happy society according to what their policy and/or constitution permits and/or commands. In general their intention is focused firstly on the security of the members of their own society and to produce and create an environment livable for their own members, and then generally for the whole society wherein their organization is formed.

They are aware of the fact that the more a society is enjoying peace and harmony there is more security for the members and the life of members in that society, and there will be less trouble disturbing their own daily social life.

It is obvious that each and every one of these establishments, organizations and sects teach, direct and advise their people to uphold the rules, moralities, proper social life and behaviour according to their aims, constitution, beliefs, as well as in line with their code of activity. To make their ideals more practical and workable and to ensure more positive results for those members in their society who follow their ideas, suggestions and laws, some of those social organizations have performed research and studies according to their own agenda. Based upon the results achieved from the research and the trials performed they have ideas, opinions, policies and guidelines that they recommend to their followers and want the followers to put those points into practice. Of course it is obvious those efforts, as well as any other attempt in this vital line of human social security, peace and happiness, are appreciated and well respected.

Let us hope more and more societies get themselves properly and wisely involved in this important moral subject and join the other honorable ones.

Establishments have recommendations based on the results they have achieved from their own studies and experiments within their line of interest and activity. Assuming societies, organizations, clubs and so on succeed to make their people adopt their laws and ethics either because those people like them or because they are afraid of punishments the question needs to be raised regarding what will happen in private, or on occasion where there is not any officer of the law and/ or responsible authority or even someone to witness and report their rebellious or improper action to authorities?

What will the situation be where there is no one to witness and prove any wrong doing of a person? What about wrong thoughts and ideas in the mind of a person? What about wrong actions in private? How can it be discovered if someone cleverly persuades a less intelligent person to take a wrong action which produces damage to the society while to this clever person it brings a beneficial result? There are many, many other questions of this kind to ask and think about.

Would obedience to the laws and regulations issued by any human organization give and render utmost success and will it be final? Or should they be changed and updated according to the changes occurring in the lifestyle and system of their society? It is obvious every society always changes either for good or regretfully to say in some occasions for bad in all dimensions and directions; thus would those previously set laws, by laws and regulations be capable and sufficient enough to keep any society just, fair and right at all times and in all aspects? Would those suggestions and laws be fully respected and observed by every member towards himself and other members in those societies; irrespective of social position, situation and condition of the person who perpetrates and commits the outlaw action?

جمله معشوق است و عاشق پرده ای

The above questions create another series of questions that need to be thought about before being answered. The question is: Does Man have to have something more beyond those laws, rules and regulations? Rules and laws he never can run away from? Laws which do not need any police or authority to watch the wrongdoings of the person, and/or keep a record of his good deeds so that he may receive suitable praise?

No law or regulation can do something constructive for the society in general and respective person in particular unless it is governed, observed and respected from inside of that person. Observance and obedience from inside the person, from his heart, is what helps and assists him to make right and honest decisions; right and proper decisions, without the influence of ego, desires and passion, instincts and self-centering. A person's egoistic desires persuade him that it is needed and/ or is necessary to ignore laws or to tell lies whereas heartfelt and sincere feeling and understanding of the laws and rules will not agree with the personal devil and therefore the person cannot perform evil actions.

Above and even beyond that is to control, train and oblige the mind—The devil of the person—to be sincere and loyal enough to accept, obey and put into practice the right advice given by the heart and take the benefit of that truthfulness and honestly.

True, honest and sincere answers to the previous questions are personal because different people have different opinions, thoughts, understandings and experiences of what is right or wrong, proper or improper, positive or negative; it is up to the person answering the questions and dependent upon their way of thinking.

Sufism or Darvish-hood's answer to the previous questions and the school's solution for the problem is simple. It is not a complicated, difficult or hard solution. The answer is practical:

When it is necessary for a person to make a decision the person, in order to make the right, best and most sincere decision, must draw upon the wisdom and the experience of his mind which is governed and directed by the sincerity, love and honesty of his heart. This consultation of both the mind with the heart will give the case perfect results.

The Maktab—e—Tasavvof and Darvish-hood, while training and directing devotees towards the Absolute Truth persuades, requests, and expects the disciples in particular, and all Mankind in general, that prior to making any decision they intend to, take their time and listen to their wise and honest conscience. Particularly at the time when they are dealing with matters concerning other people, other creatures, or nature in general Sufism humbly and kindly requests Mankind put themselves on the other passive side of the matter, then think twice, feel the results created by their decision or action and after doing such then act, decide and/or do whatever they should do.

To Hazrate Hagh, the Great Creator, all of His creatures, from the biggest to the smallest, are equal and enjoy the same rights. At the time of making a decision that affects His Creation, who is a Man to think differently or to decide otherwise?

Darvish-hood and Sufism trains, advises and accordingly expects the decision makers at the time they intend to make a decision, no matter how small or great that matter may be, when dealing with other people or when making any vital decision on matters involving others people's rights and benefits, to put themselves in the position of the other person they are deciding for, then and only if they are still happy and are sure that their decision is right and proper decide, announce and proceed with their decision for action.

All humanity is created the same, all equally beloved, with blessings bestowed upon from and by the same holy, pure and Godly love. The great source of purity, sincerity and devotion is inside everyone's own body, the closest location. It is inside their own chest, they themselves possess it is THEIR OWN HEART, and similarly is the heart of all other people.

Sufism helps and assists Man to always bear in mind this great fact that his very Creation is by love and is capable to love. Darvishes in this school of hope and sincerity are reminded that the seat of Love is nowhere else but inside their chest. Sufism or Darvish-hood teaches and persuades the people that in order to be a just judge is to consult their heart at the time of decision, since the heart is a just judge.

جمله معشوق است و عاشق پرده ای

THE JAR OOZES WHAT IT CONTAINS

Sufism's mission and the Darvish's duty are to persuade and direct Man to conduct his instincts towards the source of purity, honesty, kindness, true love and devotion. The goal, aim and the intention of this Maktab is to train and provide the disciples with sufficient knowledge and awareness of the important true source, the main spring of goodness and beauty. For them to know it IS NOT in the land of fairy tales, it is not somewhere beyond reach, located on the other side of the mountain of imaginations and dreams. Honesty, truth, justice, love and devotion are not imprisoned and/or hidden in the castle of horror, a castle protected and guarded by giants, and giants each with seven heads and one hundred horns, arms and legs.

Sufism guides Darvishes to act honestly, to love, to be emotionally sincere, to be practically and physically true and not just say moral and proper sentences constructed from hollow and empty words. A Darvish does talk about love but not by using the tongue and pouring out streams of words. What is the use or practicality of words? A Darvish is the person who performs love not just talks of love.

The school of Sufism guides and directs the Darvish to sit in a private corner with his conscience, and being sincere, truthful and honest with himself, investigate and evaluate what is the best way and best method for him to purify his mind; to challenge his selfish desires, egoism and ideas that reflect the selfishness of the untamed mind, damaging his morals, affecting negatively his asceticism, and blackening his heart. A TRUE Darvish is expected to break the crust of selfishness and to pave the way leading for Hagh's—The Truth—rays of love and affection to shine in, cleansing and purifying so that those life giving rays of His love may shine into his heart, brightening his mind thus controlling and consequently reflecting that heartfelt light and warmth through his actions and into his environment.

Sufism helps the Darvish whenever he intends to solve any problem, answer any question, and give any type of help, advice or support, whether emotional, material or physical. First of all, to be truthful, honest and attributed with Hazrate Allah's love. A Darvish before making a decision must sit alone and relax and investigate

جمله معشوق است و عاشق پرده ای

or explore his spiritual and physical condition, capacities and abilities. The Darvish must bear in mind that all capacities and qualities are granted free to him out of Hagh's love, then based on this holy foundation, pose the question and contemplate the power that he honestly has and consider the situation, analyse the pending matter and proceed to solve the problem or give advice accordingly.

As a Darvish intends to find a proper solution to a matter or render a helping hand to someone and/or serve others no matter how hard or easy that assistance may be it is his duty to ignore any passion and desire, any selfishness or ego, any expectation for being recognised and thanked. He must be calm and relaxed and consult his heart and mind, searching to find the best and most effective service and method based on the spiritual and physical capacity and ability bestowed upon him. Darvishes are to remember that those powers are bestowed on them to give service and the service should be rendered freely and sincerely to the whole of Creation, from the closest person and/or creature to him who requires or is in need of that service to a creature in the furthest corner of world needing special help. It is after these thoughts and considerations that a Darvish rolls up his sleeves and starts his job as a SERVANT.

The school of Sufism not only expects the disciple to understand the aspects of love from all dimensions, but also hopes and wishes that the Darvish will feel and even taste the glorious qualities of love and devotion which are installed in each and every one of the particles of his heart. It also does not want the Darvish to ignore or forget that for every other creature the situation is the same and similar to his. They all share similar qualities and specifications.

A Darvish has to respect the sincere and pure feelings in his heart and to understand in his mind, his responsibilities and duties for serving others. A Darvish must be honest with himself, reminding and demonstrating to his own mind that he has serious duties and responsibilities, all recommended by love and all pleasant to accomplish.

A Complete Man believes in the undeniable fact that Man is caliph and a representative of his Creator Hazrate Allah in this world, enjoying holy qualities bestowed upon him FREE and out of LOVE, therefore he as a Darvish must prove and demonstrate this fact and reality in his behaviour and actions to the utmost of his ability and capacity to himself and to other people.

جمله معشوق است و عاشق پرده ای

Sufism is the school wherein the disciples learn to act as the sun; they have to offer and give light and warmth to the lives and the hearts of other creatures, they must secure the needs of the needy people. A Darvish feels he is responsible to sincerely find, learn, practice and prepare and then present happily and earnestly to those who need assistance. His manner, ethics, wish and will is giving happiness and hope to all other people and creatures, a responsibility that is great and in the meantime pleasant. A true Darvish expects nothing in exchange for his service and help to other people from anywhere, anybody, even from his Creator God. A Darvish gives out of his heart because he feels and wants to.

A Darvish has to serve as the sun serves and grant to the needy their needs from whatever he possesses. As he is indigent, upon this unforgettable fact has therefore no right to keep anything or privilege, or reserve any right. A Darvish believes that all in his possession is given to him in order to service other Allah Almighty's creatures with. He is created to give not only to receive.

Not expecting reward and recognition is a heartfelt feeling of a Darvish that for many people is very difficult to understand. For those people more strange is the Darvish doctrine; Darvish's ethics and qualities are unbelievable, unacceptable and seem impossible to them. This feeling of love is the hardest to understand for the ego, while to a Darvish not only it is quite achievable and possible, it is a great task and mission for his heart. The feeling is so sweet that it is quite acceptable, but of course to arrive to this station of meekness it takes time, needs devotion and patience, the wayfarer arrives to this place gradually, stage-by-stage by blessing of Hazrate Hagh. What this achievement required is the Darvish's sincere and pure effort together with his Master's guidance which then receives the blessing of Hagh (Allah Merciful and Beneficent). This is a hope that seems to be very difficult but it is a hope that will be easily achievable when the Darvish is devotedly sincere, the heart is blessed and the thoughts are pure. This Darvish's constructive training started with purifying his inner self—his spirituality and morality—which in turn automatically and naturally reflected into his exterior life and his behaviour.

The true and sincere Darvish, no matter at what stage of the Path he may be must, prior to making any effort for teaching or helping other people, consult his humble and sincere heart.

جمله معشوق است و عاشق پرده ای

از کـــــوزه همان برون تراود که در اوست.

The jar oozes what it contains.

Persian Poem

OH MASTER, MAY I HAVE YOUR PERMISSION TO
INVITE PEOPLE TO HAGH?

For the Sufi or Darvish to improve and advance his morality and to have proper exterior qualities (behaviour and manner) the starting point is to properly learn and practice control over his internal qualities, then to exercise his behaviour honestly and correctly towards himself and from here, expand to all others.

It is a must for every Darvish to improve his manners in all dimensions and aspects of existence. This practice first starts from his feelings, thoughts about and towards himself and then to others which in their turn will govern his words and deeds. This is known as SOLOOK (behaviour) of a Darvish.

As the Darvish proceeds and succeeds in cleansing his mind he will deal responsibly towards himself, both his spiritual as well as his material life. The next stage for him is his behaviour towards others. Since his heart is governing his thoughts and actions and deeds whatever this Darvish does is blessed and proper. This devoted person is a positive, constructive, valuable member of the society he is living in. He will perform all positive and constructive actions possible to the benefit and for the good of his neighbour, his society and the whole world.

After a Darvish starts to exercise and practice the purification of his heart and cleansing of his mind gradually his misbehaviours give way to the proper and good behaviours that will become his habit. His heart directs him more and more correcting his dirty, black thoughts and deeds and replacing them with purity. As a consequence, the reflections of the rays of LOVE from his thoughts and actions will be evident and his presence in the society will be a blessing to that society. The rays of love, purity, sincerity, honesty, servicing, helping, rendering and giving will brighten, and warm those who are working with him.

Darvishes believe in the fact that the heart is the temple of love and devotion; to them the best behaviour is to follow suggestions and commands of their purified

جمله معشوق است و عاشق پرده ای

heart. The rays of love shining from this heart persuade and tame the mind wisely which in its turn is the centre for governing actions and the way the Sufi is going to perform what he is to do. Thus it is under such a holy climate that the disciple succeeds to think right and to make right decisions in all aspects of his life. It is then through such sincere consultation and advice of the heart that his efforts will bring happy and positive, constructive and healthy results. This sincere person's recommendations will be accepted and warmly received by other people in his society because it is based on honesty and sincerity.

Words, deeds, suggestions and whatever the Darvish makes or does for the wellbeing of his people and society will bring good and positive results when performed since he is sincere to himself that his intention is for HAGH and not to glorify his EGO.

The Darvish is reminded that he has to be cautious about the misleading of the untamed and rebellious mind and the clever tricks the mind makes to fool him. He must be alert about the potential cheating of his ego and the dangerous role his ego plays. To keep in the right direction of the Path the disciple should depend on Hagh and keep reciting his Zekr. Zekr is the proper manner and condition of the recitation of one of the names of God as instructed by a Darvish's Master. Hazrate Peer.

The higher the material place, the greater the responsibility and the more glorious the social position a Darvish has, the harder and more difficult for him to control his EGO and its tricks. Such person's responsibility to himself, his society, to humanity, and whole of Creation and most of all to HAGH is higher and more than a simple and ordinary person may have.

Once upon a time, a Darvish came into the presence of his Master; Abol—Hasan—e—Kharaghaani, and requested:

"Oh Master, may I have your permission to invite people to HAGH?"

"Yes my son," the Master replied with his usual smile on his lips, *"But on one condition, my son!"*

"What condition my Master?"

"Be cautious and do not invite people to your EGO."

جمله معشوق است و عاشق پرده ای

The above short story indicates the greatest foundation on which must be based the manners, ethics, behaviour and morality of those who believe they are invited to serve by calling other people to HAGH.

Those people who believe that they are invited or are appointed to hold a spiritual and or religious position must never forget that their duty is harder and their situation is even more difficult.

WHEN THE LISTENING EAR IS YOURS AND THE

COMPLAINT IS OURS

When a person studies the life of Darvishes, Peers and their Sheykhs he notices that his way of living, his way of behaviour towards himself and his environment is amazing. To those holy and sincere people any one of the living creatures has the same value and receives the same recognition as the next one. This Maktab teaches the Darvish to remember that all of creatures have life and their life is of precious to them, Hagh loves them and he—the Darvish—is a devotee of love and must love and respect all of them.

> میازار موری که دانه کش است
>
> *O You, don't vex that ant carrying a grain*
>
> که جان دارد و جان شیرین خوش است
>
> *That has a life, and the life is sweet.*

One of the principals in—Tasavvof—Sufism:

Do not annoy anybody or anything.

Do not disturb anybody or anything.

As a simple example, to see what this teaching means please look around you, wherever natural resources, jungles and natural habitats have been disturbed, a natural disaster has been, is and continually will be as a result from those disturbances. Regretfully Man never stops the disturbance, and it is something of which to be ashamed.

جمله معشوق است و عاشق پرده ای

I am afraid that it is too late and humanity itself is in danger of effacement before he wakes up from this sleep. A Darvish observes humankind's selfish behaviour, the wicked actions or ignorance against and towards Creation. Therefore, he advises them, points to the problems caused and warns them of consequences. The Darvish is responsible to serve Life, no matter what form it takes: people, animals, plants, jungles, mountains, rivers, oceans, inanimate "resources", rocks. The Darvish, through his heart feels the disaster which will be caused for future generations because of the selfish misbehavior of past or present generations.

> گوش اگر گوش تو و ناله اگر ناله ماست
>
> *When the listening ear is yours and the complaint is ours,*
>
> آنچه البته به جانی نرسد فریاد است
>
> *Surely what doesn't get any response is our cry for rescue*
>
> *Persian Maxim*

جمله معشوق است و عاشق پرده ای

HAPPINESS IS EVERYWHERE MAN SHOULD OBSERVE IT, SEE IT, HEAR IT, TASTE IT AND ENJOY IT.

When a person closes his eyes to deny the existence of light, he is only fooling himself and no one else since sunshine's warmth, light and beauty are there and anyone with healthy eyes, a wise conscience and proper instincts sees, feels and enjoys them. The Darvish not only happily serves good but he truly feels a serious and vital duty to eliminate evil properly and wisely from his mind; whenever a dark and improper thought or idea may come and disturb him, the true love and sincerity in his heart gets into it melts and dissolves it on the same basis as the heat of the shining sun melts ice.

The Darvish loves service to Creation and erases hatred by all of his abilities in this respect. The actions of a truly devoted Darvish are conducted, directed and helped by L O V E they are not conducted by the egoistic desires, expectations, excess passions and/or material desires and wishes.

Life is a gift from HAGH, granted through His love to all of His creatures. Life is granted to everyone but to those who are devotees to their Most Beloved, life is more than a simple saying, it is a blessing bestowed on them for which they feel grateful. To show their gratitude Darvishes must be willing to show true love to everyone everywhere. It is the Darvish's duty to help and guide other people particularly those who are unable to feel true and real happiness so that they can see the beautiful colours of life and to experience the scents of life's perfumes, to understand the reason and meaning of life, its cause and how to accept the life as they are leading and be happy with it. Since life is beautiful being productive and happy is a blessing bestowed in love upon all living creatures.

Love, of course, exists in all creatures of Creation. When someone is unable to feel the blessing and love within life, he only has to wake up and open his eyes, persuade his mind and consult the guidance of his heart to see beauty and to hear the greatest message of happiness through his heart. Surely he will see how

جمله معشوق است و عاشق پرده ای

colourful and beautiful a life is when it is conducted with Love. A Darvish's intention and effort is to be in tune with this great fact and from his heart distribute the wisdom of this love and beauty to all within his environment.

A Darvish is an ear from top-to-toe, living to hear the directing voice of Hagh. He is an eye from top-to-toe because he is to see the glorious Creation which has come into existence by the love of Beloved Hagh. A Darvish hears nothing and sees nothing but what is from HAGH; holy, pure, beautiful, innocent, happy and meaningful. He transfers, shares and pours this greatest feeling to those who need his help and assistance.

Of course people with different life experiences and conditions have different ideas and views on life; not everyone is happy with what they have, the same as not everyone is unhappy with their condition, therefore, it is the duty of Darvishes to explain to these people the ultimate of life and open their eyes to the reasons beyond every matter in life. It is a service, the Darvish is a servant, he listens, thinks, investigates, studies compares feels sympathy and then answers or advise. All he does is to consult what is coming to him through his heart's feelings, from Hagh.

Happiness is everywhere Man should observe it, see it, hear it, taste it and enjoy it.

MAN NEEDS A LOVING CORNER TO SHELTER IN

Most of the psychological and emotional problems which lay a heavy burden on the life of most people are generally the consequences of their own lack of patience, hope and positive intention. Difficulties, failures, emotional and psychological break down, desperation, hopelessness, assumption of social rejection, lack of self-confidence, and the myriad of other troubles which people think are unbearable and unsolvable, but are not something new, created in modern times. Those are the matters which Mankind has faced in the past, faces at present times and surely will face in future. They are mostly the consequences of the mind, merely the system of thinking, with nothing to do with the world outside their heart and their mind. The source of failure and or success is located inside the person. In Khaneghaah Darvish and Sufi are helped to search inside the heart and mind to find the reason which has created the problem or caused him to make mistakes, or helped him to gain success. In Khaneghaah the Sufi learns how to be patient, hopeful and positive.

In Khaneghaah Darvishes are trained not to run away from life problems and difficulties, because no matter how fast a person runs away, the speed of those bad times is faster and will catch up with him sooner or later. The more the troubled person struggles, the grip of difficulties will be tighter and more painful. A Darvish's intention is to learn to be calm, relaxed, and quiet in all aspects of their life and to welcome all of life with wide open arms; with all of its ups and downs, good and bad, right or wrong, fair or totally and completely unfair. It is more productive to calmly and wisely look into the difficult situations and find the way to eliminate the causes of grief and problems.

Man needs a loving corner to shelter in, search inside his heart, and value his existence; and to Darvishes, Khaneghaah is that corner.

Khaneghaah is a spiritual, emotional and moral shelter for Darvishes, at the times when an overwhelming problem attacks them. Khaneghaah is the house wherein Darvish takes off all of the exterior ornaments of society and surrenders. During

جمله معشوق است و عاشق پرده ای

difficult life situations Darvishes shelter in Khaneghaah and in its holy atmosphere first dismantle themselves and hope to find imperfections and eliminate them, all and completely. It is by talking honestly with himself, quietly reflecting and while relaxed, analysing the reasons regarding the existing problems (thoughts, ideas, wishes, desires, expectations, and sorrows) that a Darvish finds the answer.

According to the Maktab e Tasavvof and training of Khaneghaah, a Darvish loves everyone and everything therefore a Darvish, according to his belief, must never hate, dislike or reject anyone or anything. He must receive them in love. While using his heartfelt and sincere love he investigates and studies their problems, difficulties and expectations and decides about the way to deal and treat them still in love and with love.

Troubles and sadness, problems and difficulties, grief and hardship as well as happiness and pleasure are parts of life that no one can avoid. Therefore a wise person wisely investigates and divides his troubles into portions and sections, those smaller parts may be dealt with easier than the whole huge trouble. By sub-dividing the problem it will decompose much faster. This is the minimum benefit a person may receive from the teachings of Khaneghaah, and the Sufism. This is the shirt of the happy man.

ABU SAEED ABU AL KHAIR

According to the biographies and history books, particularly those written by his grandson Mohammad Lotf Allah and his cousin Mohammad Ebn-e—Noor Aldeen Monavvar (mostly referred to as Ebne Monavvar) his full name is Abu Saeed Fazl Allah Ebne Abu Al Khair, also known as Peere Meyhaneh, and he was born on the first of Moharram of 357 after Hejrat in the town of Meyhaneh in North East of Khoraasaan state, 75 Kilometres from the city of Sarakhs.

Abu Bul Khair, his father, was in favour of Sufism and whenever he found time he attended Sufi gatherings, but Abu Saeed's main influence towards the Path of truth or mysticism was his mother, and he always referred to this great blessing from his mother with pride and happiness.

There is a lot of information available regarding his education and the religious teachers, including the various places he went to in order to achieve benefit from the teachings of each one of those teachers. However the point we have to take from this information is that during this time Abu Saeed was not in constant and close contact with the Khaneghaah as he was during his childhood and it may be assumed that he was missing those personal spiritual ties.

Ebne Monavvar tells the story:

Abu Saeed came to city of Sarakhs, and joined the disciples and Darvishes of Abu Ali Zaaher when at this time he was teaching religious laws and religious stories (Hadis) and it was at this time that Abu Saeed again joined the circle of Darvishes. The person persuading him was Loghmaane Sarakhsi, who was famous and known as "the frenzied wise', who took him to Abol Fazl Mohammad Ebne Hasane Sarakhsi, (who died in 404 After Hejrat.)

Life went on as such and he was spending his time in his own Khaneghaah at Meyhaneh, or in Sarakhs with his teacher, until one day the teacher ordered him to go to Neyshaabour and to see Abu Abdul Rahmaan Salmi (d.412 A.H.) who

جمله معشوق است و عاشق پرده ای

bestowed upon Abu Saeed Khergheh Ershaad the garb and permission to teach and direct devotees to the Path. When he returned to his teacher Abol Fazl said to him that he had completed his teaching and he need no more of his teachings and added that from now on he should start his own duties as a Sheykh. This surprised Abu Saeed, he felt too small for such a great weight of duty; however he made endless endeavours and did his best in preparing himself for the job.

Later on his son Abu Taaher told his disciples what Abu Saeed said to him about that hard period of time.

"I was continually saying O Lord it should not me, please save me from me. I was crying blood from my eyes, and I knew nothing of myself at all. Then things changed, and I came to understand that it is not possible through performing so much mortification and self-discipline to achieve anything or get anything. It is God's Blessing which grants and bestows. It is Him and not me, so I repented from any existence . . . . When and after you completely observe your religious law it will not happen, to feel this. While you exist your infidelity exists. While He is but you assume that you also are, there exists two, and this is infidelity. There exists only ONE, you should vanish."

When Abu Saeed arrived at this point of non-existence he became the head of the circle of devotees, and it happened that no matter if friend or enemy, almost all were absorbed or attracted to his behaviour, ethics and morality. Pilgrims from the far most corners came to his Khaneghaah to meet him and enjoy his teachings; his neighbours were returning to good manners and leaving their previous wrong doings and rejection of religion. He continued:

"I was so sincerely accepted that people were coming to me to repent . . . . And then God directed and showed to me that it was not Me at all, I was nothing, and the light hit me and then I was REJECTED by people; everybody, all of those who already had accepted me and followed me. It came the time that wherever I was passing the people claimed that that piece of land was cursed, and in the mosque some women came and splashed excrement on me, and men stayed out and claimed they would not come in for their Friday prayer if I was in the mosque."

Everything and everybody were rejecting Abu Saeed as a person.

جمله معشوق است و عاشق پرده ای

In this situation he makes a bibliomancy from the Qur'an, wherein he quotes from Chapter 21 verse 35 and 36

كل نفس ذائقه الموت و نبلوكم بالشر و الخير فتنه و الينا ترجعون

Every soul must taste of death. And We test you by evil and good by way of trial. And to Us you are returned.

و اذا رآك الذين كفروا ان يتخذونک الا هزوا اهذا الذی يذکر آلهتكم و هم بذكر الرحمن هم كافرون

And when those who disbelieve see thee, they treat thee not but with mockery: Is this he who speaks of your gods? And they deny when the Beneficent God is mentioned.

Holy Qur'an

Thus Abu Saeed happily embraced whatever was happening and never complained.

When Peer Abolfazl passed away, he regularly visited his shrine, and then he visited Abol Abbas Ahmad Ghassaab in Amol, to accept his hand as his Peer. It is said that from the beginning Abol Abbas knew about his spiritual level and loved him accordingly. A story has been told about their final meeting:

". . . . And disciples saw that Sheykh Abol Abbas put his own cloak on Abu Saeed and wore the cloak of Abu Saeed himself, and it seemed to me very strange and surprising and they were amazed by that. After this Sheykh Abol Abbas turned his face to him and stated: Go back to Meyhaneh and stay there for a few days until the time that this sign be installed above the entrance gate of your residence."

Abu Saeed returned then shortly after that Abol Abbas passed away.

Abu Saeed, while being bestowed with the highest spiritual feeling, was not considering himself anything but one of the ordinary members of Khoraasaan

جمله معشوق است و عاشق پرده ای

province. At the times of teaching and preaching he was using the same simple ordinary language spoken by the people, using the vulgar folkloric idioms and poems that were used and sung by people at the ordinary level. Abu Saeed in choosing folkloric poems had been choosing the popular ones speaking about matters such as; pleasure, joy, drunkenness, languishing, advice, counsel on morality, philosophy.

It is a vital point that this very important method of training and teaching about whatever makes people more pure has been a custom for teachers in Iran from times even before the Sassanid Dynasty. In those periods poems contained the admiration and glorification of the most beautiful Beloved darlings and were extremely popular. Sheykh Abu Saeed knew the level of knowledge, understanding and acceptance of many of those people who were attending his assembly and was taking full advantage of those poems; it was to the taste of those people attending.

In the course of time, gradually whatever was recited by Abu Saeed, was sung and repeated by ordinary people on the roads, particularly those poems containing advice and teaching morality and human ethical behaviours. In fact the way the Darvishes perform and uphold their meetings, the music played and the poems recited, are based on the same foundation.

Evidently Abu Saeed's method of upholding and programming his gatherings was strongly opposed and rejected by some scholars. On one occasion when in one of his meetings the Sheykh was reciting from the holy book of Qur'an, he omitted the verses where the Book speaks about Hell and punishment, sticking to the verses which promises and gives the good news of forgiveness, praise and happiness. Someone protested and asked the reason. In reply Sheykh recited:

ساقی تو بده باده و مطرب تو بزن رود

O Cupbearer thou get the goblet round

and thee the musician play the harp

تا می خورم امروز که وقت طرب ما ست

So I drink wine, today, which is our happiness time

می هست و درم هست و بت لاله رخان هست

Wine is and money is and the tulip face idol

غم نیست اگر هست نصیب دل اعدا ست

But is no sorrow if there is fall to the lot of enemies

Persian Poem

He added: The good *news of forgiveness is our shares and their share is torment and punishment.*

It also is said that in Neyshaabour, Sheykh Aboo Abdollah Bakppyeh (Baba Koohi Shiraazi) visited Sheykh. He usually used to ask his question in the form of a protest, thus he asked Abu Saeed.

"What is this which has not been seen from other Sheykhs but you do? You place youngsters opposite elders, and grant high jobs to small ones and you do not make any distinction between senior and junior. And the other is you permit youngsters to enter into Samaa va Raghs?"

Sheykh asked: *"Is there anything else?"*

جمله معشوق است و عاشق پرده ای

And he said: "No."

Then Sheykh Abu Saeed stated:

"The matter about juniors and seniors; in our eyes and our point of view, there does not exist any junior, anybody who enters the Path even if he is junior, should be observed as senior, since whatever was granted to us in seventy years can be granted to a junior in age within a day. And when a person has such a belief he will not look down at anybody. But regarding your question about juniors dance; young people have soul as well as passion. They have passion and to mortify passions it is a highly important and vital fact that when young people clap and hit the hands together, the hands' passion is eliminated, and when they dance and hit the feet, the feet's passion is released and reduced. When they join the dance the excess passion and energy accumulated inside them is released in proper way. If this does not happen they will be under pressure and not allowed to dance, then God forbid that they may get involved in great sins and improper actions."

Sheykh said when a person is at samaa—dance—for each samaa his heart should be alive and his passion dead. The way the Iranian Darvishes start their Samaa, they start with quatrains and music. It is evident from this explanation of the Sufism of Iran, that when the school creates perfection and eliminates (to the maximum degree possible) the imperfections in people, the ego finishes and dies. It is such a high and acute position that Darvishes cannot see anything but Mankind; no religion, no nationality, no colour, no education and no social position. Man and only Man. This school is to help people to search inside and find this L O V E.

Shafiei Kadkani in (Moghaddameh Asraar Al Touhid page 231) writes that:

"The gates of Abu Saeed's Khaneghaah not only were open to the poor and needy, labourers and farmers, peasants and similar type of people, but those gates were wide open to those who were rejected by their society. His Khaneghaah was always a place for those who were rejected by the society. Thereat this Khaneghaah they were welcomed with open arms and they enjoyed the highest respect irrespective of whom or what they seemed to be."

According to Ghazveeni, the great historian, in Abu Saeed's Khaneghaah if a person felt that they needed the blessing of Abu Saeed's Khaneghaah's humble food then they were receiving two free meals per day, whether needy or those people who were considered to be well off.

Long before the religion of Islam arrived in Iran, the Iranians believed in generosity, manliness and chivalry. Abu Saeed embraced those qualities and included them in Khaneghaah teachings, making them the qualities a Darvish must have. This founded the Khaneghaah on such a great foundation that it is still the same to this day.

Prior to the time Abu Saeed established Khaneghaah in Iran there were three different systems of public places that existed which he amalgamated together. Based upon all of their beauty and usefulness he planned and established the foundations of his new kind of Khaneghaah.

1 – Rubaat (or inn): these were places or buildings wherein soldiers and border guards rested. Later on those places became used by Sufis when they were travelling or wanted to gather together.

2 – Khaneghaahs: were used by Darvishes as guesthouses where they stayed, rested and ate in when travelling around.

3 – Places established by pure, humanitarian people on the principals of chivalry, manliness and self-sacrifice: existing in parts of Iran particularly in Khoraasaan, which provided hospitality, helping the needy, sheltering and defending pilgrims.

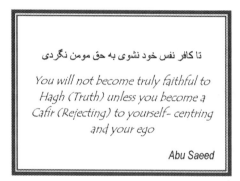

تا کافر نفس خود نشوی به حق مومن نگردی

You will not become truly faithful to Hagh (Truth) unless you become a Cafir (Rejecting) to yourself- centring and your ego

Abu Saeed

جمله معشوق است و عاشق پرده ای

Abu Saeed, by amalgamating these pure, proper, humanitarian based services added further moral and spiritual points and founded the new system of Khaneghaahs which still operates up to the present time on the same principals and basis.

Another foundational Abu Saeed rule, one which should be one of the most important teachings for the human race is his command to Darvishes that everyone must get involved in a job and social activity; no one is allowed to separate from society, or choose a remote corner and spend his life there while he is depending on other people for his needs. A Darvish is productive and renders services; Darvishes are not parasites to the human society.

He was the one who collected Iranian laws and all chivalrous manners and behaviours, amalgamated them together and founded the Khaneghaah rules.

When Abu Saeed wanted to leave Neyshaabour for his home town Meymaneh, he commanded Darvishes as such:

- ❖ The gates of Khaneghaah are to be kept wide open

- ❖ Entrance, well swept and welcoming

- ❖ The lanterns and lamps must be lit

- ❖ All hygienic regulations fully carried out.

- ❖ When someone visits Khaneghaah and provided he is capable, it is better if he comes not empty handed (brings something to contribute).

- ❖ Welcome the needy and meek with open arms and smiling faces not grievous and sour faces

- ❖ All eat together and share their food (each person to have his share individually).

- ❖ Residents in Khaneghaah are not permitted and should not ask the guests where they come from or where they are they heading.

❖ They should prepare a praying place for the guest and offer it to them with happy serving faces.

The rules are known as Abu Saeed commands, and seriously obeyed and sincerely carried out in Khaneghaahs all over Iranian territories. It was the seventh century A.H. that Majd Al Deene Baghdadi translated them into Arabic language and they became international Khaneghaah rules.

Abu Saeed, as it is preserved in the book "Asraar Al Touhid", believes that Jahaad Ba Nafse (the endeavour and act of striving hard against the ego and self-centering of Mankind) is one of the most important foundations for Sufism, and a Sufi or Darvish has to blame himself for any wrong and improper thought or action. Abu Saeed passed away on the 4th day of Shabaan (eighth months on Muslim calendar) of four hundred and fortieth year A.H. in Meyhaneh.

جمله معشوق است و عاشق پرده ای

THIS ENEMY IS THE FLAME WHICH KEEPS

MANKIND'S LIFE WARM AND ALIVE

In Khaneghaah Darvishes are taught and expected to learn how to identify and locate the cause of their own problems. On occasion Darvishes are also trained to help to solve the problems of those people who come to Khaneghaah to receive help by trying to find methods to correct the mistakes and determining the best method to eliminate those troubles.

According to the teaching of Khaneghaah, a Darvish is not only responsible to look into his own problems to identify the reason, and to eliminate the cause and thus solve them. He is a servant of the whole of humanity, thus a Darvish must consider other people's problems as his own. A Darvish is to feel the difficulty or grief others are suffering from them as their own.

But Sufism helps a Darvish to find the relevant and proper cure for any condition that people may suffer from.

Darvishes, under the supervision and teachings of the Khaneghaah, learn and understand this vital fact that self-centering, ego, greed and unachievable desires are the main causes of worry, grief, troubles, disputes, quarrels and of course, crimes. Many psychological illnesses people suffer happen at the time when they fail to get a material object or when they have cast their wish on something but it is either impossible or hard to achieve.

When some people do not achieve their wishes for material desires and luxury things, it is the time their mind becomes troubled. Gradually this feeling becomes so heavy and unbearable to them that they lose their patience and nerves; then they become aggressive, impatient, and angry and hate anybody and anything they believe is a barrier in the way of their success. These people do not think that the actual wish is improper or that it is something unworthy to think about or wish for. In fact they wrongly believe there has been a failure somehow—by themself or others. In reality it is very different. It is the ideas and wrong thinking which is causing them psychological, mental and even moral difficulties and sicknesses. The duty of a Darvish when coming across this type of people is to help them to open their mind to understand what they truly are wishing for and what beautiful and valuable time and energy are being lost chasing that improper desire. This service is another one of the Darvish's MIRACLES.

In Khaneghaah Darvishes are helped to understand the reality that the enemy of Mankind is not standing on the opposite side against and fronting him face to face, the greatest enemy is inside the skull of the person. This enemy will never be completely and totally destroyed because as long as a man is alive this enemy lives with him too, it is a part of his existence, a major part of him, he is born with it, lives with it and goes to grave with it. The Mind is a great servant and assistant in the service of an intelligent, wise and powerful governor and a dangerous enemy against a weak, undetermined, and unprepared person. It all depends on the person and the way he governs his mind.

A Darvish in Khaneghaah is trained and taught to be alert to understand, analyse and neutralize the harmful actions of this enemy. This enemy is at home as long as the person is alive; his mind lives with him with only one desire; to challenge, oppose, mislead, and fool him if he is not the right master for it. This enemy cannot be destroyed, or removed, it will not go away, for if it does the person loses all of his intelligence, intention, passion, wish, and love for a real and proper life. This enemy is the flame which keeps Mankind's life warm and alive. No one is interested in having a dead, cold, dark and ugly life, and it is not what Hagh commands. If the serving flame is not controlled the result is a disastrous fire.

To the experienced Darvishes Khaneghaah is not considered to be the only small place where they get together to be trained, to meditate and concentrate, to meet and see each other, to find about each other's problems and difficulties and or to share happiness together, to them the whole world, the whole of Creation is Khaneghaah. It is holy, it is meaningful and it is the place to serve.

جمله معشوق است و عاشق پرده ای

THE LANGUAGE OF LOVE AND DEVOTION IS AN INTERNATIONAL LANGUAGE

No society can progress unless it is founded on the best practical system of moral, right ethics, contemplation, devotion, respect and perfection. Other systems survive for a short period of time, but those systems or ideas, being founded on material purposes without consideration of human nature, respect and cooperation, morality and dignity, aren't good to anybody, and are bound for destruction. You will see it for yourself when you read the history books, read the holy books, or ask your elders to tell you stories of honest and dishonest people and organizations in society and their final destiny.

The Darvish gives preference to other people's requirements over his own and the welfare and convenience of other people over his own needs. This is one of the first, foundational and constructive steps in Solook (Darvish's behaviour towards others).

Darvishes must observe very closely and sincerely the high moral qualities throughout their daily life. Those qualities and characteristics may seem strange to people who have either not had the opportunity of knowing and experiencing the ethics of Darvishes, who have not tasted those high qualities, or those people who are lacking pure spiritual and passionate love and devotion inside their heart and mind. For some people, whose egoistic desires are stronger than their moralities and love, it is not easy to find or accept the creative and positive reasons beneath the Darvish mentality. Some people like to talk about those high qualities but it is hard or impossible for them to feel, observe and put those high qualities into action. For all of those people a Darvish must prove his claims and convince them by action, not by his tongue. Sufism is to be a living example of the truth and not only talking about the truth. Writing books, poems and saying sweet and nice words does not fill the hunger of a needy person, he needs sincere material action.

Historical records show Caliph Moatazed's Vizier sent Noori a leather purse full of gold coins requesting him to distribute among the needy. Noori put the coins on a large tray, placed in the centre of the Khaneghaah, and then he called needy people and asked them to come and take according to their needs. One took one hundred, the next something less and the other some more, till all of the coins were taken.

Then Noori said to them:

"I now am going to reveal a fact about your way of thinking, to tell you what the level of your faith in your creator Hagh is. The distance of your heartfelt feeling from Hagh corresponds and is equal to the number of the gold coins you have taken and your closeness to your beloved Hagh corresponds to the number of gold coins you seriously were in need of but you avoided and refrained from taking."

The Darvish feels responsible for the proper progress of humanity in all of its physical and spiritual dimensions. With this goal in mind he carefully studies and researches to find the best method to help him to be successful in the particular purpose he is involved in. The Sufi will search for and study all honourable heartfelt methods that he believes will help to guide him to choose the best way by which he, in his turn, may help the progress, advancement and improvement of all dimensions in his society. Sincerely, the mission is to render heartfelt service to society which, in its turn, brings positive and constructive results, the results of which the moral advancement and progress of society completely depends upon.

In line with the directions of the Maktab, the Darvish happily joins any group of any number of people who honestly and sincerely intend to help serve the progress of their society and improve in all honourable dimensions. In leading and directing the volunteer team, he should never forget that everyone in that team, just like him, is working towards that holy goal of SERVICE and fulfill the position to the best of his capacity.

The Darvish should never forget that all of his actions and services MUST BE based on SELF DENIAL and self-sacrifice:

- ❖ Any action which has its roots in ego and/or longs for any kind of recognition and/or gratefulness has no moral and spiritual, emotional and heartfelt value at all.

- ❖ A Darvish is a lover of Truth and sincerity he is not a slave of his instincts and/or desires.

جمله معشوق است و عاشق پرده ای

- ❖ The opportunity given to provide service is more valuable; above and beyond all material rewards or recognition most people expect and look for.

The generosity of giving abundant, pure love and unconditional service towards everyone and anyone are a few references to those principal manners and numerous moral qualities expected from a real and truly devoted Darvish.

Sufism prepares a Darvish to observe his daily life, behaviours and actions as if he is observing them through the eyes of Hagh and the way Hagh expects him to act as such:

- ❖ Honestly

- ❖ Sincerity

- ❖ Self-denial.

Therefore, he makes those qualities the principal foundation for any decision, action, opinion or expectation in life and or expectation in life.

The proof of sincerity and honesty is real love in action, not hollow, cold words. Simply, words are of no value at all.

The language of love and devotion is an international language, even animals, and plants understand this language.

Truthful is the one who practices truthfully and not the one who merely talks about truth.

As a Persian poet says, a Sufi becomes all Him—Hagh—and He fills all the existence of the devotee. Thus he does what Hagh wants.

As described before, Darvish-hood and Tasavvof's teachings are to be followed and observed in daily life seriously and sincerely. Those teachings are guidelines for a true and positive and beneficial life, productive, tranquil, relaxed and griefless, and generally a heavenly life. Those teachings should be mixed into the complete existence of the Sufi.

جمله معشوق است و عاشق پرده ای

اعضاء وجودم همگی دوست گرفت

The beloved grasped all of my organs and limbs,

نامی است زمن بر من و باقی همه اوست

All is Him I am only a name

Persian poem

WHY IS LOVE BLIND?

It is said; LOVE IS BLIND. Is this a good and positive reference or a bad and negative one?

Is this saying referring to LOVE as constructive or destructive?

If LOVE is the Elixir of life, If LOVE is GOD. If LOVE is the basis for all and every candid and sincere moral ethic, then WHY LOVE IS BLIND?

Have you ever thought about that?

HAVE YOU EVER BEEN IN LOVE? I trust you have, we all have been in love, are in love and will be in love. You were born in love, you were in love, you are in love now and you will continue to be in love for ever. We also, have been loved, are loved and will be love to the last breath of our life.

Then how can love be blind?

How do you describe the feeling? How can you explain that feeling? The way most people describe love is usually short sentences such as:

- ❖ It is gorgeous
- ❖ It is beautiful,
- ❖ It is fantastic
- ❖ How can I describe Love?
- ❖ Impossible
- ❖ Holy, Godly, Heavenly, pure, glorious

جمله معشوق است و عاشق پرده ای

All the above and thousands of other answers you may have come to are all correct and right, real and true.

Yes LOVE is BLIND, and in order to prove this fact; please close your eyes for a few minutes, what can you see? If someone came into this room quietly, could you see him? Do you know who he is? Is this person a friend or not? How does this person feel about you? Does this person have positive, negative or neutral feelings towards you? Honest or dishonest, beautiful or ugly, short and or tall? Educated or not educated? If they bring some furniture into the room, do you see it? Do you know what have they brought in? What the colour, design, quality, size or their material is?

If an animal enters the room, can you say if that is a lion or a horse, a tiger or a donkey, a wolf or a lamb, or what?

With closed eyes you cannot see what is happening in the room, even though you may feel there are things happening, but you do not know exactly what. You are not definite about changes, to you all of the things which have happened are unknown including the unknown animal—you are not afraid of them no matter if they are lion, tiger, wolf, dog, goat, calf, or any other harmless or fierce animal.

While in that room with your eyes closed a few people come into the room. You feel their arrival but you do not know who they are or what nationality, sect, creed, size, gender or colour, they are? Are they beautiful, handsome or ugly, you cannot say, if they are all well-built, healthy, sick or what?

Then when you do open your eyes everything will suddenly change, yes, you can see, and as soon as you see, you will start judging, measuring, valuing, deciding, for and against each and every one of them, the lion, the horse, the tiger and the donkey, the wolf and the lamb.

Then your judgment and consequent decision about the people who have entered the room, you will see who they are, whether you know them, are they familiar or strangers? When seeing the people you will immediately make distinctions between them, this is red and that is yellow, this one is white and that is black, look at that one—what a handsome man he is! But that man, how ugly he is! This lady has expensive jewels on her, but that one is so poor. This person seems to be polite and well-mannered while that man is a peasant, this lady appears to be well educated

جمله معشوق است و عاشق پرده ای

but that one is illiterate. Finally you will think I like this person, I am not sure about that other one, I do not think about that one, and I dislike that one over there.

Anyway your decisions, judgments, consideration, etc. etc. when you can see takes shapes and happens.

Now you see what the The main reason it is said LOVE IS BLIND

Love is blind because love extends to everyone and everybody. Love is blind because it does not distinguish between this and that. Love is blind because it does not choose; love is blind because it does not give advantage and privilege to one against the other. Love is blind because does not see hatred, dislike, anger, cheating, dishonesty; love is not even familiar with those words and qualities, behaviours, habits, customs and ideas. Love knows Love in the same way as sugar knows sweetness, sugar is sweet it cannot be bitter. Similar to the fact that something which is bitter cannot be sugar, it is the same for Love. Any feeling which is out of bitterness, hatred, and dishonesty is not LOVE.

هرچه گویم عشق را شرح و بیان

No matter how much I describe love,

چون به عشق آیم خجـل گردم از آن

When I come to the Love, I feel ashamed.

Moulana Rumi

جمله معشوق است و عاشق پرده ای

MASTER-HOOD IS NOT A WORLDLY POSITION

Sufism helps the Darvish to eliminate whatever weakness, egoistic desires, temptation, improper passion and self—centering he faces inside his mind. The weakness may reflect on his way of life, controlling his manners and actions in daily life. Sincerely observing whatever Sufism teaches and recommends to the Darvish will have direct positive results in his services and behaviour to the society where he resides. This social result is the first and smallest benefit the wayfarer receives from his devotion.

Peer or Morshed, Teacher or Master is the person who is indigent and meek, selfless, self-deprecating, without any pride. Ego or material desires, worldly expectations and pride, are all controlled by the feeling of his heart and teachings of the Path. He is the one who never expects to be praised, who never thinks of honour and pride, does not expect to be dealt with as a creature from out of this world, seated above all the Creation. He controls his passions, egoism, desires and wishes; his instincts are quite healthy and physically strong but under his full command and control.

A study in the biography of previous Masters and teachers in this Path is the best evidence to prove this.

We have to admit that regrettably there are some people who use a holy title such as Master, Teacher, Peer, Morshed or Sheykh to wrongly name themselves. Those people are the people who have been or are deceived by their ego, their pride, their material desires and wishes. Gladly their number is ignorable.

A Master or teacher is the person whose thoughts, passions and ego are under the strict control of his innocent heart. This Master or teacher has already travelled and revolved at his own pace in the Path to the Truth and still is and will be continuing this migration out of selfishness and egoistic desires towards Hazrate Hagh until the last breath of his life. Such a devoted and sincere person at this part of his material life is at a position from where he and or she is capable to assist, help

جمله معشوق است و عاشق پرده ای

and direct other Darvishes and interested people, the people who are willing and are prepared to surrender to this Master's teachings and hope to walk under his guidance, supervision and direction in the path to Hagh (The Truth).

In case someone wants to explain the mission and duty of a Darvish and the Path of Sufism in simple few words is to say: This School directs and conducts, helps and guides the willing man who intends and wishes to purify his soul and spirit as well as his consequent manners and conducts, irrespective to the size and amount of his position and or condition.

Sufism to the best of conditions available and capacity of the person teaches him, trains and persuades him to be a true and real human, to give priority to his sincere heartfelt expectations, wishes and good desires, the two valuable and important qualities which are the foundations of changing from the wrong direction into the path to truth and sincerity. This change of direction is the start and foundation for cleansing and polishing heart from the dust of this material world and in consequent to that control thoughts, decisions, judgments, manners and commands of mind influenced by the dust of imperfection. This purification, refinement, brightening and ornamentation changes the wayfarer from an ordinary material person in to a sincere, truthful, servant for his fellow humans, as well as all creatures in creation irrespective to their nature, quality, position, condition and or appearance.

This school of love and devotion, meekness and indigence is always well prepared and ready to welcome and assist newcomers warmly with a bunch of aromatic flowers of love and devotion. It should never be forgotten that this school is always eagerly prepared to serve interested and willing people, irrespective of their sex, age, education, knowledge, position, rank, race, belief, wealth or whatever considered high or low in the material world of today.

In the Order, Teacher (Master), Morshed, Peer, and His representatives Sheykh, Peere Daleel, are doctors, surgeons, nurses, and other serving authorities.

A doctor is for the sick patients, those who are healthy and well they do not need a doctor, so they do not go to him. Khaneghaah is a hospital for those who do not feel 100%.

The Path is similar to a restaurant in that only healthy food for both the heart and mind is served sincerely, honestly and by a truthful Sufi Master who is not solely a teacher. The Master in reality is head servant and waiter who pleasantly and happily waits on those who call for him and his team of servants to help and to assist, no matter who are ordering; their need and his service are all that is important.

The Master is not only a head servant to the stranger who requires service but he may be called to serve his disciples whenever his disciple needs and wants his service. In fact the Master has to serve his disciples and followers first and then others. They are the embedded patients in Khaneghaah—the hospital—they are to be served more intensively. There are very important and serious reasons behind this e.g. if a Master ignores his disciples then they may lose heart, becoming unwantedly and unexpectedly confused and leave the Path. The Master is the symbol and example of devotion and service to his disciples, if he shows ignorance, anything wrong can and may happen to those who have completely surrendered to him and are following him. The Master renders his service and help by love and happiness. The Master is the highest in experience, knowledge and wisdom and in the meantime the lowest in self-priding, self-centering and ego.

The Master walks with the pace of the disciple as if he is one half of the Darvish's existence. He walks the Path with the disciple, suffers the troubles with him, enjoys the happiness with him, and makes the life in Sufism for the wayfarer Darvish understandable and practicable.

A Sheykh is a Master to teach, meanwhile a SERVANT to serve and help.

The Sheykh walks with his devoted disciple while the disciple is being sheltered and protected by him however, from the moment the Hazrate Peer—Master—feels that the disciple should be left alone, because he is capable to continue his voyage independent of anybody else and depending upon his own ability, the Master softly and gradually pulls his direct assistance aside, persuading and directing his disciple to continue on his trip alone.

The Master's responsibility is as father and guardian of the Darvish. He protects and guides him up to such point where the Darvish's heartfelt and wise mind is prepared enough to continue in the Path to The Truth alone and under the light of his heart's wisdom, fully protected and guided through the Love of Hagh.

This Darvish, by the blessing of Hazrate Hagh, may too one day be a Master. She or he may one day receive light from the Absolute. This devoted person may one

جمله معشوق است و عاشق پرده ای

day be commanded to become a responsible teacher or a Master to other wayfarers and devotees, to guide them, to help them, to direct them, to hold their hand and pull them up out of and from the pit of ignorance and darkness. This meek person may be honoured to be a servant, to save others by guiding them out of the life they currently live.

It is not an easy task for a person when he feels he is responsible to serve as a Master, to serve others with the same love and dignity his Master served him with. The Darvish who reaches the point that he is commanded to that service should never ignore his high responsibility. This Darvish must never forget that as long as the smallest grain of egoistic thoughts, self-centering, selfishness, passion, desire, demand, pride and hope for position, public acceptance, recognition and respect, hope to receive financial and material presents and gifts is still alive in his mind he is not worthy for that high service. In fact his thoughts are worth nothing.

There is huge difference between guidance and invitation of Hazrate Hagh, and the cheating of ignorant NAFS (Ego).

Where a person thinks he is commanded to help other people but in his mind he has expectations for reward he should go to his corner, close the door, and seek Hagh for direction. He should remind himself that he is confused and the earthly material lust is governing his mind. It is in his own benefit to listen to the love, wisdom and truthfulness of his heart and not the knowledge of his mind. He should repent and continue cleansing his heart (the heart and mind that regretfully are under the control of the egoistic desires of his devil mind) clean his heart from the dangerous devil which is threatening his spiritually sincere life. This person has to hold the skirt of the holiness of his Master, repent from his sins, and start discipleship from the beginning, with the hope that this time he is capable of controlling his devil mind. He must learn more and being sincere enough to know his condition and position, stay there as long as his Master commands.

Master-hood is not worldly position, a person is not a Master to be respected, receive financial or material benefits, social position and whatever it may take to satisfy his earthly desires.

The Master must be down-to-earth, happy to give, ready to serve, happy to forgive, easy to forget, prepared to ignore, eager to help, always on foot to serve and interested to assist.

Darvish-Hood or Sufism is a school always present and prepared to help those who wish, hope and have the intention to purify their heart and mind. Sufism helps, directs and assists the devoted person to cleanse his complete existence from unnecessary worldly and materialistic desires, passions and egoistic wishes no matter how big and or how little those may be or seem to be.

To a Darvish, either a nave Darvish or the highest Master, the size and appearance of earthly and material thoughts and the desire of instincts are not what should be considered and regarded as important. The nature of the idea, desire, wish or intention is what makes it matter. Worldly desire, egoistic expectations, illogical passions and expectations are most ugly and they should be regarded as a serious sickness, be considered as a problem and need special attention and special care. In order to help and handle this important sickness, to cure and eliminate them properly and wisely requires adapting a simple and easy method to take hold and cure them of any other improper habit, custom, wish and wrong way of thinking.

A Sufi or Darvish who is living in society feels responsible so he does his social duties as an honest member of his society. This person practices and carries a normal life as every sincere person does; he works, earns honestly, spends responsibly, eats, drinks, sleeps, enjoys, experiences grief if and when unhappy moments occur, and takes benefit from all of his senses, instincts and feelings while under the direction of his hearty love and devotion thus responsibly conducting a healthy social life in close connection with his society.

A Darvish enjoys all proper advantages and offerings of his society but only to a point. What makes him different from many of the other people is that all of his giving and/or receiving is founded upon the purity of his heart and sincerity of his mind. His point of view and intentions are all revealed in his actions and behaviours.

A Darvish, while conducting a life somehow similar to the life of other members of his society, does not have a connection or heartfelt attachment to the material advantages in life, or the worldly possessions, or position in society that he is responsible for. In spite of the fact that many people regard the possessions or positions to have high value and interest he looks at them as the means and equipment for leading a more healthy and helpful life in this world.

The Darvish's code of ethic and aim in life is to love, to serve, to offer, to give, to forgive, and to have sympathy with everyone who is in need or requires anything.

جمله معشوق است و عاشق پرده ای

- ❖ BUT NOT TO SHOW OFF.

- ❖ NOT TO EXPECT ANYTHING IN RETURN, and

- ❖ NOT TO HOPE FOR RECOGNITION.

A Darvish does not think about, compare with or investigate the person who needs his service or help. The devoted Darvish believes in serving and giving the needy person who is in need. A Darvish's first duty is to render service, so gives and serves, and never thinks who the receiver of his services is. A tool in the hand of an experienced tradesman never asks what job it is going to be used for. The duty of the tool is to perform its duty properly according to the decision of the tradesman, the Master who uses it. Darvishes believe that the role of all of the creatures in this world is the same as the role of tools which are made to serve particular purposes and special services. Darvishes perform their duty according to what it is expected from them. The case, reason and type of the job are beyond their capacity. Hagh has created them and Hagh gives them the job according to His decision, they are to be the tools and follow the command.

To a Darvish everything has a valuable and important reason beneath and beyond existence. Why? The answer is simple Hagh created everyone and everything for a definite reason; therefore to a Darvish who is a devotee of his most beloved Hagh every matter is important because it is His Creation.

A devoted Darvish is sure that there is a great reason behind the Creation of anything and everything. Darvishes believe that based upon this sincere foundation when a duty is handed to them, no matter how great or small, positive or negative, constructive or destructive that job may appear to them, their first duty is to act sincerely and honestly, to perform the job to the best of his ability. Reasoning and questioning is beyond them. Almighty God, Hagh, has given life to everyone without consideration or expectation or hope for any return, it is out of His gracious blessing not the right of the creature.

A Darvish sees the world the way Hagh wants him to see it, not the way his ego and passion his knowledge and experiences command him to see and wish. He sees everything plain, without any colour, the same way as his heart does and his mind has to do accordingly.

One Foundational pillar of Darvish belief is to never forget that he is a humble servant of Creation and not a Master for Creation; therefore, all thoughts, deeds, behaviour and actions or reactions of Darvishes are founded on this glorious way of life.

The role of a Darvish in this world at all times has been is and will be service, service, and service; all based upon sincerity, honesty, humbleness, and Love.

The sincerely devoted person hopes to improve his thoughts and direct them to be proper, honest, sincere and pure; the person who hopes that he may finally become a better person a real Sufi or Darvish; the person who hopes that one day he succeeds to become so pure that he may become A COMPLETE Man, will act and practice love and devotion throughout his life. The serious and honestly sincere person does his best to control ego and self-centered passionate desires and selfish thoughts under the supervision of feelings of the heart. This person practices right and proper actions and always does the best to eliminate whatever barrier is in the way leading to Hagh—the Truth—the barriers such as material wishes, desires, pride, jealousy and expectation for recognition and reward for his services. A devoted Darvish is continually alert and careful against his selfish and improper wishes for gaining pride, or social respect.

A Darvish is a person to whom a venial, tiniest and smallest amount of sin e.g. to hurt, annoy, offend, disrespect, ignore any one, is a dreadfully unforgivable and unacceptable sin. To a devoted lover of Hagh, those sins are considered to be the biggest and hugest of sins, the sins which are so heavy they cannot be carried morally and are heavy enough to break the backbone and shoulder of his pure, sincere emotions and feelings.

He must avoid any kind of sin as it is too heavy a load to be carried by a person with sincere hearts and cautious morals.

To a Darvish any kind of sin is heavy and unforgivable therefore; any sin of any nature and reason has to be highly avoided and repented, even if that is just a dark thought. On the contrary a devoted person is to consider any one of his services little and ignorable. A devoted Darvish always forgets his services, while he never forgets his mistakes and sins. To those who register their name in this school this system of considering sins and services is one of the first teachings and lessons they receive in the Maktab e Tasavvof.

جمله معشوق است و عاشق پرده ای

Sufism ethics and code of practice help to practice, purify, cleanse and advance character, manners, behaviour, thoughts and desires in all aspects and dimensions of existence, purifying them to the point that a person may become a proper perfect human being. Once a person arrives at this purified station he will be capable and ready to start his journey upwards to that high point. From there he cleans off all imperfections and leaves behind his material desires and ego thus he becomes nothing earthly, he gets out of his lust, ego, selfishness, and interest in worldly wishes and desires, and keeps all of those temptations under the strict control of his heart, wisdom and holy knowledge.

When a Darvish succeeds to reach this point the present condition of his heart and position of existence is the point that is a reliable base for his next level of purification. The Darvish starts ascending towards such a high position that he becomes worthy enough to be absolute nothing, to be dissolved, submersed and a simple drop absorbed, annihilated in the ocean of love and devotion. This great change of emotions and manners is similar to a drop of water at the time the drop reaches the ocean and dies out of the life of a simple ignorable drop and joins the glory and greatness of the ocean; there will be no more a drop, because then and there everything is just one and only ocean. That tiny little ignorable drop now is the greatest of the great Oceans.

The above is the condition of the true man when he has reached the point that is worthy enough to be one with the only ONE. When the drop surrenders, dissolves and loses the EXISTENCE as a little drop of water and yields its identity as a drop it becomes the everlasting, eternal living OCEAN of LOVE.

For a Darvish whose hope and wish is be annihilated and dissolved in the love of Hazrate Hagh similar to that drop, it is vital to lose his lust, ego and individual existence, thus he becomes not as an individual but as the ONE.

Unless the drop dies out of its existence, it will never become one with the ocean. Drop will remain a drop and stay a drop until it evaporates and finishes—that will be the end of the drop. That will be complete non-existence, death.

A Darvish has to die out of all of his material desires and wishes. He should die out of his 'I', the crust and shell of his egoist, self-centred desires and wishes. He has to come out (which is not an easy task) to become united, merged and become one with his glorious darling Hagh.

جمله معشوق است و عاشق پرده ای

The teachings and guidelines of Sufism direct and help the devotee to cleanse inside his heart, the heart that is the temple of Love. They enable the Darvish to purify his mind, as when the mind is not controlled by the light of love and devotion it will become the seat of the misleading devil. This purification and cleansing is not an easy task, but it will be possible through directing, teaching and guidance of Darvish-hood and Sufism.

The key to this precious treasure is surrendering to the guidance and directing of Hazrate Peer.

خلـــوت در انجمـــن

Solitude by own heart while living with society

One of Darvish-hood's principals

Darvish-hood and Sufism serves, directs, assists, persuades and guides the Darvish to become a sincere honest servant for humanity and through all of his inward and outward existence—his heart and thoughts, deeds, actions and behaviour, be of sincere help and assistance to everyone, acting honestly towards the whole world. A Darvish does his activities sincerely and completely for Hagh, not for material desires and expectations.

A Sufi or Darvish always shows his happy appreciation to whatever he receives, no matter how large or small, cheap or expensive that thing may be and who the person giving it may be. Darvish believes it is a present from another's heart to him so it is blessed and gracious.

It is the responsibility and duty of Sufism to assist the devoted disciple of the Path to control, eliminate and to demolish the thoughts of an uncontrolled mind, and the consequent actions. The School of Sufism directs, teaches and trains Darvish to reconstruct his existence through love, love for anyone and everyone, love for all of creatures as one global group. The Disciples experience sincerity and learn to love everyone without any distinction, without granting any advantage or privilege to one person over another; similar to a lover, who, when admiring his Beloved

جمله معشوق است و عاشق پرده ای

loses himself completely and becomes love, the Darvish becomes Love, to love the most Beloved Deity from top—to—toe. To a Sufi, humanity is one body therefore he loves this body from top-to-toe. To the Darvish everybody is a Doost—Friend and beloved and there is a Sufi proverb which says:

هر چه از دوست میرسد نیکوست

Whatever granted by the Beloved is right.

Sufi proverb

Sufism is the school wherein the devoted person learns how to reject and denounce selfish desires and any kind of attachment to worldly possessions. Tasavvof directs and persuades new Darvishes how to practice to be indigent, meek, and humble. In this school Darvish learn how to be a person in physical appearance exists and lives physically as any other human being or other living creature does, while beyond that as a Sufi he always remember he is non-existent in his passions, desires, pride, material and worldly wishes and egoistic demands.

The school teaches to the disciple practical methods to control his desires and for the wish for the material and worldly assets. Tasavvof makes the Darvishes familiar with the fact that the spirit of greed, pride and carrying egoistic passions and desires may not and will not survive and exist in the field of Darvish—hood. A Darvish is completely effaced and non-existent in any field of self-centering and lust. He does not want or wish to have anything for his own well-being and sake, to satisfy his material desires and happiness. All a Darvish wishes for is not to have a wish; to be content with what has been provided for his being by Hazrate Hagh.

درویش آنی است که نباشد

A Darvish is a person who does not exist

Traditional Darvish saying

جمله معشوق است و عاشق پرده ای

The person who thinks that he is intending to practice the guidelines and teachings of Sufism but does not observe, follow and obey, practice and put into positive action any one of the above duties towards himself as well as other creatures is only a dreamer, a pretender and not a true Darvish in the Maktab e Tasavvof.

جمله معشوق است و عاشق پرده ای

HEART AND SOUL

خواجه عبد الله انصاری در رساله دل و جان چنین فرماید

بدان ای عزیز که زندگانی بر مرگ وقتی ترجیح دارد که این چند
چیز نگاه دارد

O my dear, Beware that life is preferable to death if and
provided the following qualities and points are
observed

اول با حق سبحانه و تعالی به صدق

First: Honesty and Truthfulness to Hagh – Truth- the
Glorious and the Most High

دوم با خلق به انصاف

Second: Deal fairly and justly with people

سوم با نفس به قهر

Third: To be rough and tough to self-passions –
mortify passion-

چهارم با مهتران به عزت

Fourth: Respect Seniors, greater (elders)

پنجم با کهتران به شفقت

Fifth: kindness to juniors (younger).

جمله معشوق است و عاشق پرده ای

ششم با دوستان به نصیحت

Sixth: To friends admonish.

هفتم با دشمنان به مروت

Seventh: To enemies with fairness.

هشتم با درویشان به سخاوت

Eighth: To the poor by generosity.

نهم با جاهلان به خاموشی

Ninth: Silence against ignorant

Khaajeh Abdoolahe Ansaari, "Heart and Soul"

Let us ask ourselves and answer to ourselves honestly; if each and every one of Mankind obliges to practice and observe the above points could there be left any space, possibility and position and/or grip left in mind for ego, self-centering, dispute, anger, jealousy and envy? Surely the answer to the question would be NO, Not at all.

جمله معشوق است و عاشق پرده ای

WHY CONDEMN THE WEAPON AND NOT THE

HAND THAT PULLS THE TRIGGER?

A gentleman who is about 75 years of age, together with his adorable wife who is about 73, came to visit us. They were from one of the towns in North Queensland and this gentleman seemed to be quite healthy, a true sports man, happy and, according to him, financially well off in their life. Both wife and husband adored and admired each other and their love was pouring out of their eyes and from the smiles on their lips. They said that they had travelled quite extensively around the world and have seen many people and places. The gentleman told us that he is a successful farmer and his family is truly healthy and happy. This man, while telling the stories about his personal experiences around the world, told a beautiful and meaningful story which is relevant here. He said:

"During one of our trips, we visited a local pub and came to meet a group of people who were concerned about their town's problems. They were discussing the crimes and misbehaviour of people and the causes of those improper actions. They were talking about how they would prevent all of the existing and progressing violence, crime and hatred occurring; determined to find a solution. Most of the men and women were condemning alcohol and alcohol consumption. They had strong reasons for their comments and were quite serious and passionate regarding what they believed to be true; although it is interesting to note that while they were all so seriously interested to solve the problems, they themselves were under the influence of considerable alcohol. Despite this, they were sure that when alcohol is banned, the townspeople will have a trouble-free life; there will be nothing to cause aggression and they imagined a happy, safe, crimeless, just and livable town.

I waited and waited until they had all given their ideas and presented their case (all opinions and comments stated strongly and very passionately) and then I said:

"WHY DO YOU CONDEMN THE TOOL AND NOT THE HAND WHICH USES THE TOOL?

جمله معشوق است و عاشق پرده ای

WHY CONDEMN THE WEAPON AND NOT THE HAND THAT PULLS THE TRIGGER?"

Wrong doings, mistakes, bad and improper manners and actions and finally crime—they are not in the alcohol, they are in the mind of the person who commits them. In most cases alcohol is innocent; why do you crucify alcohol? If a person does not have the capacity to consume alcohol then he should not drink. But where he does ignore his capacity and drink and consume alcohol and then, under the influence of that drink, commit a crime he has to accept the consequences and be punished for his wrong doing. To keep your society safe and secure, that is a moral responsibility for each and every one of you. You must teach and train members in your society to distinguish between wrong and right, good and bad, safe and dangerous, pure and evil. Where someone still persists, in spite of the training, and does not have the capacity to drink, but does drink and then behaves improperly then it is the right of your society to give them what the person deserves; the person has to face the consequences of his wrong doing. Eliminate the cause and the consequence will be eliminated automatically."

When an unpleasant situation or a bad luck falls on the head of a victim, he immediately condemns the whole world but not himself, he considers everybody else guilty, but not himself. As in the above story, condemning alcohol and not the lack of proper, right manners and character in those who drink the alcohol. Why do you condemn the tool and not the hand which uses that tool?

The victim, who is the criminal and wrong doer, is not truly in control of his hand, or even beyond that. It is not the hand and not even the person; it is his heart and mind and decisions made wrongly that created the so called crime..

جمله معشوق است و عاشق پرده ای

A WISE MAN ALWAYS ELIMINATES THE CAUSE

From the first day of Man's existence in this world and surely continuing to the last day that the Mankind exists on the surface of this earth, every man has, is facing and will encounter numerous problems and difficulties in life; this is a natural part of life and inevitable. On this foundation it is obviously vital for any person who encounters problems to know the best method and the proper way to face those problems, to accept them as they are and find the best possible method to solve them with minimum effort and less energy, and in the shortest time. It is quite natural, proper and normal that people expect that they should overcome their problems and difficulties by finding practical methods and ways to solve them easily, or at least expect to pass through unpleasant and difficult periods eventually.

For the troubled person in order to conquer the situation he is facing it is essential and vital to observe the difficulty, think carefully about that and its consequence, and then decide accordingly while both relaxed and calm.

When an entangled person wisely analyses his problem and decides thoughtfully to control the situation it is by being well prepared and powered by hope, and equipped and armed with strong determination, that the hard period or event has no choice but to gradually and slowly dissolve.

The heart of Man through its love, sincerity, holiness and wisdom is already well equipped and prepared to encounter, face and solve the material problems and emotional hardships the person comes across. The main barrier and negative force that prevents him to positively act, solve and get rid of those difficulties is the mind. Problems appear to be much bigger, stronger and frightening particularly when the person is under stress and emotional pressure. Since the capacity of any mind is limited, the knowledge and experience is bound to that capacity and therefore is not strong or capable enough to perform suitable functions properly or make the right and correct decision.

جمله معشوق است و عاشق پرده ای

It is on this occasion that the training and teachings of Sufism come to the aid of the entangled person. Those teachings and experiences remind him of his abilities, persuade him to have confidence in his own abilities and to keep calm and be relaxed. Under such cool headed conditions the troubled person decides to overcome the situation. This is the minimum constructive promise Sufism has for people, but the most vital step for the person is to make a positive decision and pay attention to the messages and encouragement.

Trouble and difficulties are a permanent and also constructive part of life; they always exist to make Man stronger, more experienced and knowledgeable. Their help is vital because to take a further step upwards is not easy and requires interest, proper preparation, experience, intention and also the ability to solve problems and confusions. Who is the person who is capable to take the first step and to complete this job in minimum time and with minimum energy and achieve most benefits? The answer is simple: He who accepts the advice given to him by teachers, elders and all of the other people who have more experience in the matter. The successful people are those people who accept the advice given to them.

To solve those unexpected conditions and difficulties the person has to have patience, must be calm and tranquil, over and beyond this the person should be armed with determination and have the power and ability benefiting from the wisdom and knowledge experienced and collected in his lifetime. It is through education and experience that it becomes possible for the person to make right and appropriate decisions. All of those qualities are normal qualities laid in Mankind and expected from each and every intelligent and wise person to benefit from and put them into use, but how? And how many people are capable to do so? How many people are strong enough that at the time of need act with knowledge, calmly, properly and wisely? Is everybody capable, wise or strong enough to have his emotions under strict control and encounter the problems he faces relaxed, dealing with them the way they have to be dealt with?

The answer to all of the above questions is not easy but it is certain that not everyone is strong enough, patient, and wise enough to face difficulties with power and wisdom. Many people usually panic and consequently make hasty, wrong or improper decisions. They need help, guidance, sympathy, understanding and the right amount of assistance. A sincere devoted and loving Darvish is the sympathetic person who up to his capacity and ability is ready with friendly open arms and heartfelt feeling to assist the person in trouble. This is the starting point from where

جمله معشوق است و عاشق پرده ای

the responsibility of every devoted Darvish begins. The Darvish starts his duty by giving and helping happily and eagerly offering and doing whatever in his power, he can to help and assist the person, those people or the society in need of proper, right, and practical advice.

The school of Sufism is not only the right place where people learn and practice the ways and methods to use their abilities and patience. However the Maktab teaches people the proper method to remain tranquil, relaxed and calm when confronting any unexpected accident or unpleasant occasion, while wisely benefiting from their wisdom and experiences. Remaining calm and tranquil is necessary to help the person at the time of trouble. But also in the second stage it is required to help people to benefit from their own wisdom and experience as well as all of problemsolving knowledge, experience and qualities which in most cases the person in trouble ignores and forgets about. Wise, sincere and heartfelt analysing of the attacking problems, assist the person to choose the proper method to face that expected or unexpected situation and solve it comfortably. To be successful the person has to carefully search for the main reason beneath the troubles which he is facing and try to eliminate that cause and reason patiently and gradually, step-by-step.

A wise man always eliminates the cause and the consequences will fade away by themselves.

At the time of trouble and hardship the most important factor to help the entangled person out of the danger and damage is to not to lose patience, not to panic and not to be agitated because a mind under such weak condition will never help. A confused mind will not be capable to get rid of the cause, on the contrary only makes the situation harder and more difficult.

Man should be strong enough to benefit from his wisdom. When a person does not do so, his knowledge and mind not working properly to assist him, he is incapable of finding a proper solution for his problems and difficulties; no matter how big they look to be or how they appear and/or they seem to be unsolvable. Among his personal qualities are his patience and his power to wisely analyse the situation with his mind's sincere cooperation and obedience with his heart and moralities. Sufism helps Man to wisely connect his thoughts to the love from his heart and through cooperation between heart and mind (Spirituality and material knowledge) honestly analyse and solve the problems. The results he achieves from this investigation will enable him to choose the right and proper solution, the best and right method or way to deal with encountering problem or problems.

It is evident that the mind (knowledge and intellect) always analyses matters, prepares and reports the results achieved to the master (Man), then after this it is the next duty of the mind to recommend the most practical solution to the person to make a proper and workable decision based upon those results.

What is explained above outlines the duty of the mind to properly and sincerely function but since the mind is a material component of Man it normally suggests and persuades its master to choose a decision suiting a material benefit for his life. It usually persuades the person to choose the decision which is only in his own interests while ignoring and forgetting totally and completely the benefit or rights of any other. Normally the mind wants the person to ignore the privilege of other people and/or parties involved. This means that though the decision of the mind and the suggestion it makes is for the benefit of the person in many cases that decision is not founded on sincerity and honesty. The mind considers its decision to be right because the decision is only for the benefit of the person's material and temporal benefit, to free him from a situation, to make a bigger profit, to gain benefit which in most cases to both the mind and the master seems to be proper, right and correct.

Does the heart's honesty and sincerity agree with that decision or does it consider that there is another important matter that should be considered and decided about honestly?

In cases as such, experienced as well as new Darvishes are to carefully consider and analyse the comments and/or the decision of their mind. They very sincerely and seriously should consult their heart, observing wisely and honestly the case from all aspects neutrally, accurately and seriously in order to find what or where should be the firm base and foundation on which they are going to make their final decision.

جمله معشوق است و عاشق پرده ای

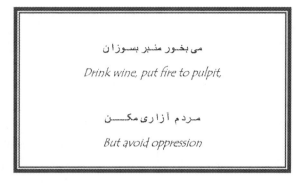

می بخور منبر بسوزان

Drink wine, put fire to pulpit,

مـردم آزاری مکـــــن

But avoid oppression

The duty and responsibility of experienced Darvishes in this case is much higher and intense. They must give very close and keen attention to all facts and even beyond that. All Darvishes experienced or not, are expected to sacrifice their own rights if it honestly is for the benefit of other people's satisfaction and happiness. This seems to be a difficult decision and the consequent action is not easy, if not impossible for most people, however a Darvish and Sufi is obliged to deal with the matter in this way.

A true and sincere person who hopes to become a Darvish is a person who is always prepared and willing to give happily with an open smiling face. While in exchange he does not expect or wish to receive anything.

According to the teachings of the school of Sufism, a devotee has to choose the fair and proper solution for the problems arising in life, this solution should be based on fairness and honesty. Whatever the decision of this person is it has to be right and proper and to the benefit of the other parties and not unjust and unfair to others, one sided or merely for his own benefit. An experienced Darvish has to give, to surrender and leave all benefits for other people particularly when they need them. Sufis live, serve and wish the best of the best for all other people with truth and sincerity, through their heart and not egoistic wishes.

In all cases, from the smallest cases to the largest, the greatest importance in one's life to the experienced Darvish is that it is not their duty but their right to make their decision based in favour of the other person while ignoring their own personal profits and benefits. The person in love with the Most Beloved never considers any material profit for his own.

A Darvish must give advantage and privilege to other people over himself, it is a must and the GOLDEN RULE as the code of ethics for all whether experienced or inexperienced Darvishes.

A devoted Darvish reminds his fellow humans that any decision and/or action to solve the problems in daily life based on ego, ignorance, selfishness, are not proper and honest, even if they submit some temporary satisfactory results for the person deciding, that result is temporary and fades fast even though it makes him happy or satisfied. To a Sufi to damage, to hurt, to endanger, humiliate and disrespect others is the greatest sin, and this sin to him is unforgivable and unforgettable. A decision not based on sincerity and truthfulness will not provide absolute and final results. The satisfaction or pleasure achieved in this case will be short term, while consequences will remain and surely the end result will be extremely horrible for him. Any hasty and improper decision made not on the basis of self-control and honesty would produce for the Darvish, as well as his Beloved, damage and grief. The hardest consequence to himself will be a burden on the shoulder of his conscience for the rest of his life.

The decision a Sufi makes MUST be based on his self-sacrifice, to grant and give privilege to other people's interest over his own. To him success is the smile he sees on the face of the other person, the person receiving the privilege, a reward so gracious and precious and impossible to buy by anything material.

On the above basis the person who has registered his name in the school of Sufism, during all hard and difficult occasions is expected to be tranquil, calm, wise and alert. A Darvish must be well aware that it is his duty to act towards any matter on the basis of love and understanding as if he already had been expecting the unexpected and so he is already prepared to accept and deal with it.

The Darvish believes that any improper decision will have unpleasant consequences and could bring damaging results on the material, social, emotional and/or spiritual life of himself and/or his fellow humans, therefore, in order to avoid any damages caused by mistakes it is best to avoid mistakes. It is a moral duty of a Darvish to persuade other people that when they face any difficulty not to lose their control, not to panic but on the contrary use their own wisdom, knowledge and experiences or take the advantage and benefit from the knowledge and wisdom of those other reliable experienced and honest people.

جمله معشوق است و عاشق پرده ای

A Darvish is not allowed to be careless about the life and future of others

Those people whose intention is to become a Darvish, before registering their name in any school or order, should crack the crust of their self-centering, worldly passion and desires, surrender their spirituality, thoughts and physical existence and abilities completely to Hagh—without any resistance, ego or passion. Under this heartfelt and sincere condition the person is out of the complete control of ego, selfishness, wishes, desires and passion and his thoughts, actions and behaviour will be neutral towards different matters, thus he may be positive, proper and better prepared. A successful devotee knows that he will not succeed in gaining any achievement in the direction of surrendering his material, egoistic desires unless he successfully controls his desire with the complete supervision of his determined and honest conscience.

Sufis to the best of their ability eliminate their selfish improper wants, expectations and passions and dismantle their egoistic desires wisely, sincerely and completely. Where there is someone who is unwilling or disinterested to intend to do as such, it is better for him not bother to register in the school of Sufism.

It is easy to register in this school and wear a garb and cloak, carry a beggar's bowl and stringed rosaries, have an axe in hand and a crown on the head. However it is difficult to be a Darvish in reality. A true Darvish, when a decision is to be made, does not have any personal desire, passion and wish for profit, benefit, prize, appreciation, recognition, and social position favour or hatred. In fact Darvishes teach themselves and train themselves to always remember that they have no right to want and/or expect anything of any kind which may satisfy their desires and fool their mind by its material glory. Darvishes must remind their mind that even though they do exist materially any egoistic desires do not exist in them; their wish is a heartfelt wish for other people's happiness. Thus it is far beyond a Darvish to wish things for his own glory, pride, well-being and worldly position and possession.

بار کج هرگز به منزل نخواهد رسید

The crooked load will never reach the destination.

Persian Proverb

جمله معشوق است و عاشق پرده ای

Darvish is a person to give and grant, not to get and receive.

Darvishes believe that the heart of any person is the palace for the glorification of the Most Beloved, The Most High and Beneficent and the real temple for His love and the Darvish himself is the servant of that high temple. With this glorious reason a Darvish highly values himself as well as all of the other people and creatures. The Darvish conducts his life sincerely and in the meantime humbly. A Darvish never forgets that he is the guardian of his heart, the temple of Love, and as the servant for all of Creation he humbly respects other people.

A devoted Darvish does not wish, want or expect anything, all happiness is in his service and the better he serves the more happiness he has. He wants to give and wishes to succeed in offering happiness and satisfaction to other people. What reward is as valuable to one who has such purity and sincerity?

A Sufi must follow Sincerity, Love and Devotion. He must follow the most positive method and way to crack completely the crust of self-centring, wrongful passion, jealousy, anger, cheating, lying, and any other sin and spiritual or moral crime one can think of. The teaching of Maktab e Tasavvof is to direct people to come out of their evil condition and serve their fellow humans with dignity and sincerity, to offer and give to the needy with love, and to receive whatever is given to him with thanks, and prepare to give it again to the needy.

Sin is born within and grows by the attention of ego. A Darvish believes that the mother of all sins is strongly nestling in ego, which nurses the improper behaviour of self-centring, the existence of wrongful passions and selfish desires, the wanting of all things for the ego's benefit, expectations of glory and recognition, improper habits. Maktab e Tasavvof teaches the Darvish to avoid surrendering to those sins, preventing any wrong doing. To do all the right things to ensure the control of mind from the improper hands of ego means to control and convince the mind wisely in such a manner that it agrees with his master (The Darvish). In this important respect the mind must understand and surrender to the Darvish as he is purifying his inward and outward departments. The Darvish wants to be a servant to Creation without any expectation; he intends not to exist materially and to have no wishes at all. When a person does not exist how can his ego influence his life? How can any worldly desire tempt and persuade him into doing wrong and cheating himself?

جمله معشوق است و عاشق پرده ای

A Darvish who is poor and indigent believes he does not require or need to possess anything for himself in this school—the school of devotion and service. The disciple is convinced that he does not even exist, and cannot entertain the desire to have worldly wealth, possessions, wishes and desire for anything material.

All of those people who honestly and sincerely intend to travel towards absolute Truth, they believe that all of the wealth, material properties, conditions, social positions and authority they may have or hold is granted to them by Hagh to serve Creation; they are responsible and have authority over those materials and powers to use them for the service of the people. A Darvish's code of ethics tells him that he is to serve other people, not that the people are to serve him.

A Darvish must fulfill the job definition and position requirements no matter what position in society he has. He must also serve everyone entitled to the maximum of his capacity. If he is in a position to do so, the true Darvish that holds a higher position with authority over people must not forget that he has to tame his ego, melt out more and more of his material desires and passions, feel more responsibility towards the people he is supposed to serve, and satisfy the regulations designated for the position he holds. A Darvish must teach to his subordinates that all of them are obligated to do the same and accept the heavy responsibility.

Even if a Darvish possesses the wealth of the whole world or holds the highest social position this does not give him any moral or spiritual superiority over any other person; his social condition should not create any material pride, self-satisfaction and happiness. His duty is to responsibly make the best benefit out of all of those facilities and possibilities for human society, the society that he himself belongs.

Whatever possession a Darvish is enjoying, if and when it slips out of his ownership it should not affect him, his life, and his faith, harm him emotionally, and make him grieve, worry or be sad. He should be wise enough to believe that Hagh gave it to him for a reason and Hagh took it back as well for another reason.

Darvishes through the guidance and help of the teachings of the Tarighat (The Path) spiritually, mentally and emotionally prepare themselves for happily welcoming and encountering expected or unexpected problems and difficulties, troubles, and discomforts, or vice versa success, happiness, advancement, comfort and achievements which may affect them in any moment of their daily life.

When faced with discomfort, unpleasant times or conditions, if the Darvish accepts it with the belief that such unhappiness and discomfort has a reason beyond it, his intention will then be to locate the reason and/or cause in his own heart, decisions and consequent actions, his behaviour in the past or what he is doing currently. To eliminate the trouble the person is entangled with he has to erase the cause, consequently the pain will be erased automatically.

Saadi tells the following story:

There was a rich man who owned a large number of sheep and goats; the man had a shepherd who grazed the flock on the mountains and one day a wild storm attacked the area. It started raining so hard that it produced a very strong and powerful flood which while rushing down the mountain, took all the flock of sheep and goats with itself. Poor and helpless the shepherd runs to his master, the rich man, and reports the situation to him.

The rich man who had lost all of his flock and consequently a portion of his income started to weep and cry, complaining of his bad luck and unpleasant life.

Saadi goes to him in a friendly manner, with a sympathetic face, telling him: "O my dear gentleman, do not grieve, do not cry, do not be sad. This is Life. It is Destiny and not only you, but no one can overcome his share. My dear gentleman, do you remember when you were selling the milk produced by those poor sheep and goats and how much water you were mixing in with it? My dear poor man, those small quantities of water accumulated on the top of each other and became this fierce flood that washed away your flock. Don't worry but be happy that had you yourself been there at the time, you would have been washed away as well."

To encounter hard matters, problems and difficulties the Darvish prepares and equips himself with the guidelines and teachings he has received in the Maktab. These lessons and guidelines are then combined with his personal experiences from travelling in the path of the Truth, and with the advice given to him directly by his Master. These directions and guidelines help him to bear the hardship of the circumstances, find and eliminate the cause of problem, and in the meantime and most important of all learn his lesson from the situation he has become entangled in, tested and tried for future reference.

جمله معشوق است و عاشق پرده ای

I LOVE THEM FIRST AND THEN THEY LOVE ME

The teaching and guidance of Sufism prepares Darvishes spiritually, as well as emotionally, mentally, morally and materially to be alert, sincerely, honestly, truly and truthfully well-prepared and ready to defend Hagh—The Truth—against Naa Hagh—untruth.

Anybody has the capacity and the ability to be a Darvish, in fact everyone is a Sufi, everyone is a lover of Hagh—The Truth—God, Allah, Khoda, Ahoora, or whatever name you wish to call your Beloved. It does not make any difference in His and your relationship; he is the Beloved as in His Holy Book.

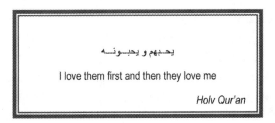

يحـبـهم و يحبــونـــه

I love them first and then they love me

Holy Qur'an

What else can or may be as promising for Mankind as this great promise? Who else or what other message or promise can give and bring happiness to Man in comparison to such assurance?

Everyone loves innocence, purity and sincerity, in fact humans are born innocent and pure with all good and proper qualities. They are born in God's LOVE and the person born in LOVE has all of the good qualities bestowed on him, what else is in this world can be compared to Love?

Much to our regret, it is time and circumstances, environment, social conditioning, and culture which affect some people and causes them to have wrong behaviour. These conditions persuade their devil mind and selfish desires to fully control and overtake their life, misdirecting them to make decisions desired by their ego. It is under such conditions and circumstances that these people completely ignore and/ or forget the holy and high qualities bestowed upon them, it is sad.

Worry, fear, unhappiness, restlessness, grief, sadness, financial pressure, and one thousand and one other bitter and life threatening conditions are causing people to commit wrongful actions. The actions not only disturb the life of the person who has committed that wrongful action, but the unpleasant consequences of such wrong doing not only affect and remain in him and his life but it usually influences and reflects on the life of the next and even several generations in whom this persons' genes are transferred to. Transient material pleasures fade while unpleasant consequences continue to exist. Isn't this a crime?

In the course of teaching the followers of the path of Hagh—Truth—the methods of guidance, teaching, and directing which Sufism uses are from the first stage for the benefit of the disciples and Darvishes themselves. When those points, directions or subjects are practiced a person who is prepared and capable to control his desires, self-centring and unnecessary destructive passions and demands, he will become transformed and become relaxed, happy and released from a pressured life. For the person whose mind is disobedient and free from the leash of love and devotion, uncontrolled by the love and sincerity of his heart, then the worldly material desires will attack his happy life and overtake the control of his manners, leaving him with the angry, aggressive desires, passions and excessive demands and have a negative influence on his honesty, sincerity and true human qualities of his heart. Such person's material thoughts will be out of control, permitting ego and egoistic expectations to overcome the mind and mislead it to make incorrect decisions.

A Darvish is the person who chooses for his existence to be governed by pure and proper principals. With the help of this intention and by sincere determination together with hard work he will achieve his constructive goal successfully. This person can be anybody, from anywhere, with any background, belief and from any sect, because for Hagh it is the intention, hopes and wishes, and the positive and constructive action of the person that are important, not his background or position, wealth or education.

Everyone is created from the LOVE of HAGH and his existence is mixed with that glorious LOVE. Yes the existence of Man is a mixture of LOVE and other high qualities, but LOVE has superiority. All qualities necessary to make Man happy are already bestowed upon him, it is up to the individual to make the proper use of them and gain benefit for himself as well as for all others.

جمله معشوق است و عاشق پرده ای

THE HIGHER HE WISHES TO ASCEND,

THE MORE DIFFICULT TESTS AND EXAMS WILL BE.

For all people it is the cooperation between heart and mind which influences the way they think either in private or public, in personal or social matters, and at the time of consideration and deliberations about others. The heart and mind influence the way people think, consider, judge, decide and act. It is the proper and sincere cooperation between them which creates the final character and personality. In short it is the harmonious cooperation of the heart and mind that governs personality, behaviour and ethics in public as well as their thoughts, decisions and judgments in private. If a person observes the guidance from his honest heart when making decisions and uses the wisdom and experiences he has collected and gathered in his lifetime, his actions will be proper and right. If he does not, then what are the results? Normally the results are not positive, are very short-sighted and of course unacceptable.

A Darvish is the same as any other person in the world. In the course of his very existence he faces different kinds of pleasant and unpleasant things, occasions, conditions and matters. However a Darvish is taught and trained to accept calmly and happily the unpleasant bundles of happenings which fall over his head. Being both calm and relaxed he encounters all unpleasant and bitter matters of life with a smiling face; he accepts and embraces these hard times with wide open arms, accepting them without complaint. Where the habits of other people may be to scold or blame others for the difficulty he is facing, a Darvish will never accuse anyone else of being responsible. A Sufi or Darvish understands that the matters happening to him and the causes thereof may prove to be different, even opposite to what he has expected and too, the Sufi knows that the cause for the unexpected unpleasantness must be searched for somewhere inside himself and nowhere else. As Saadi said to that gentleman, the small quantities of water continually added to the milk were accumulated and became a strong flood strong enough to wash sheep and goats away, why should the storm be scourged?

جمله معشوق است و عاشق پرده ای

During hard times a Darvish must remain under the supervision of his sincere and truthful heart and dig inside his mind to look for the main reason for that unpleasantness. It can be the consequence of many events, or caused by his own fault, or it may even be a test to try and examine his sincerity, or maybe the situation has occurred to prepare and strengthen his heart and make his instincts ready for ascending and advancing to higher positions and conditions. The Darvish's duty is to receive matters as they happen to him.

To ascend to a higher spiritual condition and position requires hard work and the person on the Path will face lots of difficulties, tests and trials similar to any student who is to advance to a higher class and level of education in his studies; the higher he wants to go, the more difficult tests and exams will be.

The mission of the Maktab e Tasavvof is not only to prepare those who attend but all Mankind to understand the fact that the cause for anything happening to them either good or bad is inside the heart of they themselves. No matter bitter or sweet, pleasant or unpleasant, success or failure. A Sufi has no right to complain about anything which is beyond his immediate understanding. A Darvish is always grateful for what he receives, whatever happens, no matter if he thinks it is favourable or not, he is always appreciative since there is a greater reason beyond and behind the appearances. The Darvish receives and considers what is happening to him as something similar to a Darvish examination, which proves his heartfelt quality and ability and if he has learnt what is required for a candidate to advance to higher level.

جمله معشوق است و عاشق پرده ای

THE FUNCTION AT THE HEART OF A DARVISH'S HEART IS SIMILAR TO THE FUNCTION OF A TREATMENT PLAN

Another principal duty of a Darvish is to be ready and prepared to share other people's problems, difficulties and hard times and, with them, gather as much knowledge and information so he may then investigate and find a solution for those troubles. The Darvish's action would be the same as a doctor, psychologist, surgeon, friend, partner, and a shareholder in ownership of the problem or grief or sadness of the other person. The heart of a Darvish's function is similar to a treatment plan created to analyse, treat and break into small parts the unpleasant burdens people suffer from, then to draw it out of their life.

Psychological pressure and worldly desires push some poor people to a corner and create sadness, nervous breakdown and even physical pain for them. It is of great help to those suffering people when they share the disturbing problems they have with a reliable person; a person who is ready and capable to listen to them and intends to find relief and solutions to their grief.

Many people believe that to assist such an entangled person a Darvish is one of the proper people to seek for help. Darvishes are ready to carefully listen, non-judgmentally, and give from his heartfelt sincerity a suggested method of encountering the problems to solve part or parts of the real, underlying cause of their problem. This mutual cooperation with a Darvish automatically solves all or at least parts of their trouble and helps them to get out from underneath of the heavy burden they are carrying.

When someone has a problem bothering his heart, mind and nerves, if the person decides to consult a Darvish, normally the results achieved from the consultation are positive because the guidance and frankness of that Sufi person are based on the results he has discovered through personal experience, contemplation and the teachings of the Maktab. The Darvish understands the true reasons beneath the trouble and together with the solution he can explain and demonstrate to the troubled person to assist them to understand the nature of their situation.

Once the Darvish understands the problem fully, the next step is look for all possible results of the person's situation and actions. The Darvish will assist and prepare the troubled person to accept the damage and the consequences, but this acceptance is not something heavy and out of helplessness, it is the logical acceptance that comes with understanding the real cause.

Finally the Darvish will investigate and suggest all possible and practical steps forward and assist the person to act accordingly. This is facing the truth and the reality of the situation between two of them, finding real solutions to the real foundation of the problem and sharing the burden.

This consultation, talking and sharing of the situation will reduce the pressure on the emotions and nerves of the person in trouble, and opens his eyes to the real situation he is involved in.

Darvishes are expected, as they are thoroughly trained, to listen to other people's problems, difficulties and hardships and to share the "bad luck" which has befallen the entangled person and to help them out of the misery they feel trapped in. Where someone calls themself "Darvish" and does not have the quality or capacity or is not prepared to perform the duty this person cannot be named or regarded as a Darvish but only a liar to himself and to his community.

جمله معشوق است و عاشق پرده ای

IF A MAN KNOWS THE CAUSE OF HIS SICKNESS,

CURING IS EASIER AND FASTER.

Sufism opens the eyes of people to see that beneath the majority of their dissatisfaction, grief and worries are thoughts. These thoughts are sourced from their improper desires and unrealistic expectations from either themselves or others. To be saved from such unpleasant conditions troubled people are expected to solve the problem by looking for the source inside their mind and, with the help of a professional, treat and remove the source from inside. Sufism frankly, sincerely and honestly teaches that it is Man himself who makes his and his neighbours' life and environment bright, happy, healthy and successful or dark, cold, ugly, miserable and unsuccessful. This frankness and the pure way Sufism tells the people about their life and how their behaviour affects and creates their happiness or grief is the simplest method through which this school opens the eyes and understanding of people.

After consultation with the Darvish, finding the true reason behind the problem, it may not be easy for a person to discover the cause of his troubles and unhappiness is inside his mind. He must sincerely admit that he is the one who should be scolded for the discomfort which he is currently facing. At this stage of the process the pressure on this person's nerves, mind and finally heart is less than at the start, and yes, he is in a more relaxed and calmer condition, being able to see the problems more clearly, and choosing the right and proper solution. But now, it is time for the cure.

Sufism does not claim to teach how to make miracles, like changing copper into gold. Sufism does not claim that it can teach people how to magically feed one hundred people with one loaf of bread. A Darvish will never claim that he is capable of changing the cruel enemy or competitor into a frog or stone, or a poisonous snake into a harmless earthworm. The miracle of Sufism is to open the heart of Man to understand that the source of happiness or sadness is within him and nowhere else. If Man knows the cause of his sickness, curing is easier and faster.

The teaching of the Maktab helps the person to be more realistic and broad minded, to accept life as it is with its ups and downs, how to face any expected and/or unexpected matter. Understand that life is like a bouquet of lots and lots of different flowers collected from different plants, with various characteristics; they may be colourful or plain, beautifully scented, odourless or even with an unpleasant smell or thorns. It is the nature of life and when life is viewed under this light, gigantic troubles melt down and become bearable, solvable and do not evoke misery.

When the barrier is removed, and the heart is open to accept this information, based on truth and honesty, there is great cooperation from the heart. This mind accepts that the situation is now a favorable one, the heart opens and love from the heart guides the person's actions:

THE GREAT MIRACLE HAS OCCURRED.

Happiness is not located inside a safe where people keep their gold, silver and jewelry. It is not under the seat of those with high positions and it is not placed beneath the garb of those pretending holiness. Happiness is in simply loving life. When Man sincerely searches inside his heart amazingly he will find happiness is there waiting for him to discover it.

Once upon a time there was a Queen who had a great kingdom; handsome servants, beautiful maids; her musicians and dancers were the most talented; she had a powerful and obedient army, and a great treasure full of gold, precious stones and silver. She possessed a multitude of glorious, huge palaces in different parts of her country and she spent time residing in each, according to the season and the climate.

But in spite of all of that might and wealth she was experiencing a very unhappy life. Her life was miserable, full of grief, sadness, worry, pressure; she did not have any comfortable night's sleep and no daytime relaxation. She did not experience happiness. The Queen had never enjoyed pleasure from any of the possessions or great might that she had inherited.

Over time the Queen's patience ran out and she lost the strength to withstand the situation a moment more. She called in all of the doctors and physicians from all over her kingdom to come to her presence and find a solution for her sad situation. They all arrived with bundles of books and note books, they examined her, consulted

جمله معشوق است و عاشق پرده ای

together, had long meetings but regrettably none of them could do anything positive in her favour; there was no medicine, no cure and no solution.

Her Majesty lost her faith in her wise doctors and physicians, so she commanded her Vizier to find a solution to her problem from anywhere and at any price. The Vizier investigated everywhere and . . . finally . . . one of his old friends told him that there was a very old Darvish living in a mountain cave in an isolated part of the kingdom. "I believe he has the proper solution to this misery." His friend said.

The Vizier travelled immediately to the remote mountain cave, greeted and respected the poor, indigent Darvish according to Royal customs (which surprised the simple Darvish) and informed the Darvish about his Queen's trouble, and begged him for his help to find a solution.

The old Darvish, raised his eyebrows, looked at the Vizier and in a low but strong voice said to him:

"*Go and find a happy person, borrow his shirt and let your Queen wear that shirt for a few minutes. As soon as she wears the shirt she will become happy and all of her sadness, grief and worry will disappear.*"

The Vizier bid farewell to the Darvish and thought to himself, *this should be easy to get*, and proudly galloped his horse back to the palace. Soon the town criers were calling everywhere across the kingdom, asking all of Her Majesty's citizens to find a happy person.

Finally, the HAPPY PERSON was found.

The Vizier took the Queen's men and went to the happy man to investigate. Yes he was the answer! Here was a truly, extremely, happy person. It seemed that the whole world's wealth belonged to him; he was in love with all of Creation and was of the belief that the whole of Creation loved him. He was courteous, polite, had an easy and pleasant true smile on his lips; his eyes reflected the deepest oceans of love and piety. The Vizier was amazed at this happy man's relaxed, natural beauty it seemed to him the beauty of the whole world was granted to him and bestowed on his appearance. It was the time to inform him of their request.

The happy man was told about the reason he was invited to the court of Her Majesty the Queen, and he was told that in exchange for his shirt he would be honoured to receive from Her Majesty anything he wishes.

The HAPPY MAN in reply to their request only smiled and pointed to his naked body.

Yes the poor indigent happy man DID NOT HAVE A SHIRT.

Happiness is not found in what possessions a person has; it is found in the heart.

جمله معشوق است و عاشق پرده ای

THE HAPPY MAN HAS NO SHIRT

Through teachings of Maktab e Tasavvof the disciple is taught that some of the roots of sadness for Mankind are unrealistic expectations;

❖ Expectations of a person that are beyond their own capacity and abilities

❖ Expectations from other people

❖ Material and financial expectations which are beyond their capacity and power.

A Darvish with an open and clear mind distinguishes that most of the causes and reasons for his own or other people's unhappiness are based on their ambitiousness, instinctual love, or ego and thousand and one other matters as such. It is based on his blindly following selfishness 'I'.

When the ego decides to achieve something no matter what, it cheats the person and that poor victim cannot feel and understand the way in which he is cheated. Ego works so finely and cleverly to convince him that it is vital and necessary for the happiness of his entire life to obtain the item that the poor person cannot even feel it. When the poor person cannot gain what their 'I' wants and when they experience failure, they become agitated, confused, angry, aggressive, and demanding all the while experiencing unnecessary troubles and difficulties. The person loses hope and becomes sad, then depressed, after that he will sicken and deteriorate inside and outside; possibly the person falls into the dangerous and destructive hands of addiction to alcohol and drugs or other kinds of life destroying poisons. The final tragedy is very sad, when the person, loses his heart, becomes sick, then aggressive, his colleagues lose their respect for him, most of the time he loses his position and job, and finally from a positive, energetic, active, constructive member of society he becomes idle, useless and a burden for the society. But WHY and for what logical reason are all of these troubles necessary?

جمله معشوق است و عاشق پرده ای

WHY? WHY? WHY?

Those people are not sincere enough with themselves, they are not, truthfully and honestly, prepared to investigate logically and properly, and then work correctly towards those goals. They are never prepared to ask themselves what type of consequences the expectation could bring. Yet from the very beginning this person could access the power of heartfelt wisdom, could have controlled the desires and wishes of his 'I', if he was prepared and ready to distinguish what he can afford and/or what he cannot afford. He never was trapped and facing such unbearable and troubled life forever.

Khaneghaah prepares a Darvish's heart and wisdom to ask his mind questions before permitting the mind to focus its attention on those wishes and desires. Through the eyes of a Darvish most of the passionately desired wishes and material goals are for the luxurious, less practical or necessary items useful for his daily life. A Darvish always questions himself when something is not one of necessities of life as to what reason shall a person suffer so much to achieve it? Unless something proves to be an honestly and seriously vital article without which life is impossible then the Darvish thinks he may lead his life without it. If it is vital the Darvish may decide to go for it or leave it alone as his capacity and heartfelt wisdom advises.

When under the influence of such a heavy and destructive condition if he turns to Sufism and asks for help, he will receive the help. A well prepared Darvish will be happy to help him with lots of heartfelt love and this patient will receive the medicine to his sickness. He may believe that the sickness is incurable, his burdens the heaviest, his failure the most destructive but he will be cured and in time he will get back onto his feet; active, hopeful and energetic.

Sufis believe the medicine is available and easy to get, the problem is the patient himself, because he is the one who in most cases is not interested and reluctant to take the bitter medicine. It is he who is uncooperative and inattentive to the advice and suggestions of experienced experts; ignoring the people whose intention it is to help him. Similar to a patient who refuses to take his medicine the duty of Sufism is to convince the patient to be prepared to cooperate and to be ready to take the medicine. Obliging and pushing him to it is another matter.

جمله معشوق است و عاشق پرده ای

> ثروت دنیا همسان چرک روی دست است که
>
> *Wealth of the world is similar to the dirt on the palm of your hand.*
>
> به آسانی می آید و به همان آسانی شسته شده و پاک میگردد
>
> *It accumulates easily and fast and washes away easily and fast.*
>
> Hazrate Ali son-in-law of Prophet Mohammad

The heart of the Sufi gradually and continuously opens during his travelling on the path to Hagh thus he steadily and continually learns how to excavate inside the mind and heart to discover the sources of problems, the problems which mostly are caused and created by the selfish and negative action of ego. He gradually discovers that his "I", no matter what the nature of the desires of that "I", is the first source of his problems, unhappiness and grief. To cure his sickness, to be relieved from his misery and to become a healthy and happy serving member of the world he starts by treating his own sickness with the help of the teachings of his Sheykh. This endeavour will surely have the Blessing of Hagh, thus one-by-one this person eliminates his imperfections while hoping that one day he may be A Complete Man.

From the Darvish's experience and guidance the troubled person realises that each and every human being is responsible for their own behaviour and consequences. They can see that good, positive and creative behaviour is to be continued and improved and negative or destructive behaviour is where they learn their lessons. To many Darvishes lots of people's wishes are so baseless they wonder how those people do not even consider if in their present capacity such a thing is suiting them or honestly and seriously practical or an objective to think and dream about? Is it needed or deserved? The medicine Sufism prescribes for this psychological sick person is very simple:

جمله معشوق است و عاشق پرده ای

❖ WISH FOR WHAT IS NECESSARY, AFFORDABLE AND POSSIBLE TO ACHIEVE

❖ THINK: IS IT SERIOUSLY REQUIRED FOR YOUR IMMEDIATE DAILY NECESSITIES OF LIFE?

❖ COMMAND YOUR EGO TO SERVE YOU; DO NOT LET IT FOOL YOU.

The happy man has no shirt and a Darvish has to be the happy man. A Darvish is indigent.

جمله معشوق است و عاشق پرده ای

FORGET THE BODY, YOU NEED NO SHIRT.

Desirous people do not think about the real value of the things that they passionately and seriously want to have; they do not even consider the cost they have to pay for those things or even the amount of the time and effort they have to commit to, to save enough money to purchase those articles. Most desirous people do not want to know if, under their present circumstances, they are even capable to buy their desired article. These poor people are not prepared or ready to ask themselves what type of wish they have and what would be the consequences of getting their wish?

The many reasons that people show interest and want to have something:

- ❖ to feel more important, superior and richer than another person

- ❖ to prove they belong to a certain group

- ❖ because they feel jealousy and want to compete with another relative, friend, and/or colleague

- ❖ because buying something has become an addiction

No matter how big or small, cheap or expensive the thing may be, people want to own the article, position or property merely to prove they have it.

What a funny desire.

In lot of cases the matter, position and/or object the person has cast all of his attention on so eagerly does not suit the style, method, system, and way of his living or his nature and is completely in a different category from his life. The desires do not suit him at all, he cannot benefit from them, cannot use them but still the person does not want to think about the realities and the consequences of his passion.

جمله معشوق است و عاشق پرده ای

If the desirous person held a sincere and neutral thought about his wish, it would prove that most of the luxury, decorative and ornamental items he may wish for not only are not needed, or useful but on the contrary, are unnecessary or at least not used very often. Desiring after the wish causes feelings of uselessness and failure consequently causes him nervous breakdown, psychological sickness and all other secondary physical illnesses as well.

However, even if the wished for, longed for, item is attained time goes by and that which seemed to be so beautiful and lovely, necessary and important proves to be either out of fashion or style or not of interest any more. On one occasion it was the highest desire now it has become a burden on the shoulder of the poor person who spent so much of his mind, life, time and money on it. What a pity.

Visualise the above in relation to yourself or someone you know and consider the items that you have which truly and honestly do not have any logical, or at least practical use, or those things that you had to have but no longer attach worth or value to. Do you agree that all of those consequent troubles and difficulties and attempts are the consequent results of the demand of ego, selfishness, jealousy, passion, and other shallow reasons? You can see how the poor victim pays. But WHY?

A Darvish asks himself if in this temporary and impermanent life are fading, cheap and short-lived pleasures needed and necessary. Those temporary objectives which will fade and pass as fast as a flash of light in the dark night; do they deserve so much hardship?

A Darvish asks himself is a little circumstantial, transient pleasure worth that much:

- ❖ Effort and time: finding the article, finding finance to pay for the article

- ❖ Worry: will someone steal it? Will someone have something better?

- ❖ Money: meeting regular payments, running costs, insurance, interest

جمله معشوق است و عاشق پرده ای

- ❖ Pressure on heart and mind and nerves; paying for it, sustaining it, waiting for the occasion and/or opportunity to arise to make it possible to show it off to other people

Sometimes greedy or selfish people have to put their honesty and honour under the feet of their ego, and become corrupt. They bribe, steal, cheat or one thousand and one other dishonest measures to secure enough finance to purchase what their devil mind and devil ego WANTS them to buy. What will the final result be? More troubles, more worries, more negative consequences.

Is it right to do so much labour and hard work only to satisfy ego and selfishness?

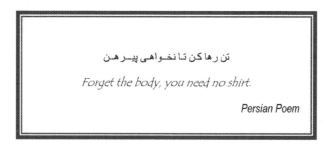

تن رها کن تا نخواهی پیرهن

Forget the body, you need no shirt.

Persian Poem

Usually the answer, as you thought, is NO.

A Darvish's intention is to conquer the power of his ego, to loosen the grip of selfishness and temptation and save his own life, therefore he does his best to take the control in his own hand, to directly steer and drive his desires and passions to the straight path of honesty and truth. The Darvish intends to be a simple, ordinary indigent and useful man, to enjoy the true natural, simple, and real life without worry or grief, happily at the service of his society.

- ❖ DO NOT obey the command of your ego

- ❖ EXPECT what you deserve

- ❖ DO NOT run after what is not vital

If you do not use this simple method to make a right and proper decision you should not be intending to be a Darvish.

طریق کام جستن چیست ترک کام خود گفتن

What is the method to fulfill desires? Renouncing desires

کلاه سروری این است اگر این ترک بردوزی

Your Royal crown is perfect when to attain it, you complete it with the quality of renounce.

Sarmad, a Persian mystic poet,

Prescription to cure psychological sickness

THE VEIL COVERING THE FACE OF MY SOUL,

IS THE DUST CLOUD OF MY BODY

Sufism teaches Darvishes to live in the real world and not in the world of dreams. The world of dreams is not reality. A Darvish lives here on the earth and not in the air with a mind full of unrealistic fantasies. A Darvish lives in society, with the society and is a useful serving member for that society. He is responsible for all and every one of his actions and reactions. A Darvish does not permit himself to have any negative or unpleasant reaction to other people's accidental or even intentional improper actions towards him; his duty is to give and to FORGIVE.

A person no matter what high position he may hold in his life and society, or how great the wealth he may have in his possession or on the contrary no matter what kind of low, simple and ordinary person he may be, he will have a happy and blessed life when he has no serious or deep attachment to his temporary wealth and position. Likewise, in the case where a person is under pressure or suffers from extensive and unbearable problems or where life is going opposite to expectations and his days are not as bright and happy as he expected, he is assured that this is temporary too.

When he believes that whatever he has only temporarily belongs to him, that everything is temporary and sooner or later will slip out of his possession to become somebody else's belonging, he will be happy. Life will not stay smooth and happy and will not stay dark and hard. When a person thinks as such, he will lead a happy life, creating a bright, happy, pleasant and affordable environment for himself and for those people who are close to him. That is all as it should be.

When a man feels responsible towards his possessions, position and properties as well as his fellows and society, when he is willingly and without any expectation forgiving others and rendering free services to anybody in need, such man is a Darvish at heart—no matter if he is initiated into an order of Sufism or not.

Darvish-hood is not a school course to study and is not a material position to achieve. It is an honour, to work towards.

Those who are the slave of their ego and are controlled and commanded by their passions and earthly desires easily become excited, pleased and happy with whatever materially belongs to them or they have control over. E.g. their wealth, possessions, and position they possess at work or in society. Their superiority to other people and those temporary advantages make them feel high and proud. Their wealth, properties, houses, cars, villas (particularly while they are new) will give them utmost pleasure and happiness which regrettably for them, lasts only for a short period of time. After a while the positions they hold, the properties, things and goods for which they have worked so hard and did so much right, and perhaps wrong, to get start to be ordinary and mundane. Again the person tries to find new challenges and toys in other places and situations; again the cycle goes on and on and never stops probably to the last day of their life. These people never get what truly and permanently makes them happy and will never be psychologically at rest because they have no knowledge of true happiness. They DO NOT KNOW WHAT THEY WANT. They have never been, are not and if they do not change their mind and the behaviour, they will never be, tranquil or happy. They are not constructive in their own personal life and will never be sincere, positive, constructive and helpful members for their society or any society. These people have to change their life, thoughts, manners and desires. For their own sake they must get rid of these bad habits and to exchange all of those for logical, workable and honest ones.

The poor, helpless person's condition is not all his fault. There are those who are close to him such as parents, teachers, partner, relatives and friends who should feel and share the guilt and blame with him as well. The whole society is to be scolded too since "they" have not done "their" share of the duty to properly teach and train this person about the reality and truth about life; and how to achieve true love and the true happiness.

If this troubled person is incapable of eliminating his desires and ego by himself, but is wise enough to find help, he may present himself to a Sheykh, Master, elder, teacher or knowledgeable person and request his help. Then the person must surrender his spiritual growth, emotional wishes and moral behaviours to the guidance of the Sheykh so that he may direct him steadily, gradually and step-by-step to the safe shores of a truly happy human life. However no matter how sincere the Master may be he cannot complete his duty unless the disciple himself

جمله معشوق است و عاشق پرده ای

is prepared and willing; it is the disciple who must determine and decide that he himself is ready to replace his ego, his personal devil, and all life threatening ideas with true and realistic lessons of a simple but truly happy life.

حجاب چهره جان میشود غبار تنم

The veil covering the face of my soul,

is the dust cloud of my body

خوشا دمی که از این چهره پرده بر فکنم

O happy shall I be the moment I unveil this face.

Hafiz, great mystic poet of Shiraz

Prescription for psychological sickness

Those people or societies which ignore their moral responsibility are speedily running downhill towards destruction. Nothing can save them because they themselves are not interested in salvation and freedom. Normally no one destroys others; people destroy themselves.

The school of Sufism's guidance and advice for those people is;

Please wake up. Please help yourself. Change your direction from the wrong way you are presently heading. Stop rolling downhill, wake up and listen to the feeling in your heart. Let true love and sincerity assist you and change your direction from selfishness and improper materialistic desires. Please consider that purity, honesty, sincerity, love, devotion and good intentions have a place in your life. Become a human being in a humane society. Leave ego behind, and love others.

جمله معشوق است و عاشق پرده ای

People who are very proud and pleased with the position they hold in their society, thinking that their position or situation is eternal, are short sighted. Those people believe that they are superior to the other members of their society. What delusion!

Regretfully that sort of thinking of superiority is simply a product of their desires which are, in origin, the grandiose dreams of their ego and passions. Good examples are those who think they are very religious people. Those people believe that they are closer to God than other people. Based upon this wrongful sense of self-importance they are sure that they are above the ordinary people of society and it is their right to look down on others. This exaggerated sense of importance becomes worse when they occupy the seat of a religious position and they receive the respect of people, according to their custom. Many people in society respect those who represent the holy and have morally responsible and respectable positions, thus the religious officiate will falsely assume it is they who deserve respect and not the seat and position.

The story becomes funnier when people paying respect to the religious representative stand back to let these "important people" get in first; or when some of more simple people kiss the hand of these people (kissing the hand is against the values of any religion). For the poor slave of ego the actions of those plain and innocent people make the situation both more dangerous on one hand and funny on the other. The actions and behaviour of those simple and kind hearted people fools these self-appointed representatives of their Lord to become ever more highly inflated with a false sense of self-satisfaction. The balloon of their ego becomes bigger and bigger containing no true prestige and honour but only wind. To add to their glory they wear special robes and garments, in this way their appearance helps them to draw other people's attention to them and prove their superiority. Some go even further and wear colourful and shiny jewelry and ornaments. Then on top of all of that they attach some strange and colourful pieces of fabric to their garbs, by which time they now completely look like some sort of clown.

Those truly deluded poor people do not know that in reality they are fooled by their several big and heavy rings on their left hand and their huge garb with all of those strange colours. The Maktab which is aware and understands their sickness does not protest to them, reject them or ban them but on the contrary with a sincere heart advises them and lovingly points out mistakes. Kindly, sincerely and innocently but firmly, the School of Sufism begs these people who honestly suffer from serious

جمله معشوق است و عاشق پرده ای

egotistic illness to declare war on their own ego and self-aggrandizement to break this false crust and shell and become realistic; to become a true human. Become FREE and come back to HUMANITY.

In order to prevent and avoid those unpleasant and dangerous occasions a Darvish does not have any right or permission to dress differently from the customs of his people or to behave strangely or differently so that he may find the opportunity to draw people's attention to himself, and thus satisfy the temptation of the ego.

To avoid this kind of mistake and selfish behaviour Darvishes or Sufis are strongly and firmly commanded to sincerely, and by honest determination and positive desires, start the complete destruction of their egotistic desires and be cautious of the fact that ego, passion and selfish desires never die but on the contrary those sicknesses always quietly and silently hide themselves anticipating the opportunity to attack the thoughts whenever the person is least expecting them.

Sufism teaches Darvishes to be honest and sincere to their own selves and find the roots of their problems inside their own mind, because when a person is honest with himself, he will be honest to everybody else and thus lots of social problems will be settled amicably. The positive, heartfelt, willing and sincere intention of the Darvish, together with the teaching and guidance of Maktab makes a Darvish's life easier, happier, and lighter. He feels that his life is always influenced by the affection, love, truth and reality of Hagh.

حجاب چهره جان میشود غبار تنم

The veil covering the face of my soul,

is the dust cloud of my body

خوشا د می که ا زین چهره پرد ه بر فکنم

O happy shall I be the moment I unveil this face.

Hafiz, great mystic poet of Shiraz

Prescription for psychological sickness

ARE YOU HONESTLY WHAT YOU PRETEND YOU ARE?

When a person is sure of the fact that he is created "good", his heart is thirsty for "good"; and upon this solid, pure and holy foundation the person trains and teaches his mind to believe in "good". Consequently his thoughts will automatically be good and he is always at peace with himself, his life and the whole of Creation; he is the true representative of Hagh—and he is the one who brightens his environment as a candle does in the dark. This is the quality every Darvish is expected to have.

Where a person claims to be one of the followers of the Path but does not possess the above qualities, he must think twice about his claim and achieve them by hard work and study to correct his life accordingly.

To declare "I AM A DARVISH", is an act and action of ego which to Darvishes is a heavy sin. The Darvish must forgive other people's mistakes, correct his own mistakes and repent for them.

Simplicity, service, reliability, truthfulness, sincerity and love are all pre-granted and nestled inside the heart of Man which wisely directs the mind of the person to proper actions if he desires so. The glory of love is not outside the person or placed in the garb or cloak. That glorious love, sincerity, purity, service and charity which grants self-confidence and happiness is inside the heart of Mankind and the easiest way to reach happiness is only to look inside.

What do those self-declared religious leaders want or expect to achieve? Why do they do so many things which have no relation to real spirituality? What truly do those people expect to gain and achieve from those behaviours? Do they honestly believe that they are true and real representatives of the Lord? Then who has given that authority to them? Are they as holy and innocent as they pretend to be? They themselves do not know and truly, we do not know.

Those pretenders of holiness in reality are poor and helpless creatures, they are sick in mind and ill in behaviour. Those people are prisoners of their material desire,

جمله معشوق است و عاشق پرده ای

passion and ego. To change their situation is up to them to take over the control of their ego by consulting with the wisdom sourced in their heart. Those poor people need serious help but it is up to them to ask.

شیخی به زنی فاحشه گفتا مستی

A clergy scolded a whore said you are drunk

هر لحظه به دامان کسی بنشستی

Every other minute you lay in the arms of a different person.

گفتا شیخا هر آنچه گوئی هستم

She replied, O your Excellency; I am whatever you address me as

اما تو هر آنچه مینمائی هستی؟

What about you? Are you honestly what you pretend you are?

Omar Khayyam

جمله معشوق است و عاشق پرده ای

WHOEVER TEACHES ME ONE WORD WILL BE
MY MASTER FOR THE REST OF MY LIFE

It is the moral duty of everyone to highly respect and honour teachers for the vital service they render to humanity. Hazrate Ali, the son-in-law and cousin of Prophet Mohammad, spent practically all of his life, while the Prophet was physically in this world, learning the spiritual, moral and social way of life direct from him, The Prophet of God. Ali had the honour of personally receiving the Prophet's teaching, supervision and Master-ship. When he was at the age of marriage and asked for the Prophet's permission, he received the permission and blessing of the Prophet to marry the Prophet's daughter. Ali has a great aphorism about the people whose intention it is to teach honestly and for the good and benefit of the receiver and not for their own worldly pride and benefit. Those honourable people definitely are the true teachers.

> هر آنکس که مرا یک حرف بیاموزد , پس او مرا عمری آقا و معلم خواهد بود .
>
> *Whoever teaches me one word will be my Master for the rest of my life.*
>
> Hazrate Ali, the son-in-law and cousin of
>
> Prophet Mohammad

Ali does not lay down any condition for this Master. He does not say if this person or that person, or a person in this position or financial situation, or a person older than me or younger than me, a man or a woman, a Muslim or a non-Muslim or Atheist, yellow skinned or white, black or red, short or tall, fat or slim. He simply, frankly and very sincerely says:

جمله معشوق است و عاشق پرده ای

WHOEVER teaches me . . . . will be my MASTER . . . for the REST OF MY LIFE.

The above clarifies how high and valuable the spiritual, moral and social position of an honest teacher is and how people must appreciate their service and help to society. It is also vital to advise here that when a teacher thinks he is higher than others, expects special advantage over other people, and thinks society has to go out of its way to make him happy and satisfied this kind of expectation is nothing but ego, which in the school of meekness is a sin. The prime duty of a teacher is to teach his pupils to be humble, honest, pure, helpful, responsible and respectable. How can a teacher himself be selfish and demanding while he is expected to teach to his pupils the opposite?

The Maktab e Tasavvof trains Darvishes to correct and purify themselves prior to teaching other people. While deciding, even prior to getting himself involved in any teaching of pupils, the Darvish must internalise the qualities he is going to teach to his disciples. He must investigate his own ethics and morals so that his words and actions match.

Even though it is the moral duty of the members of the society to respect those people who serve their society, it must be remembered that those teachers who, at the command of their ego, expect to be respected and want people to give them superiority not only devalue their own services and job but damage the reputation of other respectful teachers who teach, help and serve because of the holy nature of teaching.

Surely every intelligent and knowledgeable person agrees that the service that a good-hearted and sincere teacher renders has integral high spiritual and moral value. As for those selfish people, they should know that they are receiving their wages as salary, so the society materially does not owe them anything more. It is they who are to train and tame the ego that has undeserved expectations and demands.

Selfishness, ego and evil desires are the most dangerous enemies of Man. To a person with an untamed ego every show of respect, praise or even reward is important. To the uncontrolled ego the temporary happiness the mind gets from the respect they receive from the parents of their pupils or the pupils themselves is more important to them than the nature of blessed, pure and perfect teaching. What

جمله معشوق است و عاشق پرده ای

a lowly desire and how cheaply those people are exchanging the high value of the teaching profession with stupid selfish expectations. Oh poor people.

The Maktab e Tasavvof advises that the true heartfelt happiness is in serving other people with no expectation of thanks, or of receiving any reward or special position. The real and true value is in the Virtue. Sufism invites those whose method of thinking is different from this sincere and simple way of thinking to open their moral eyes to the facts and to visualise the beautiful reality that to honest, sincere and honourable teachers whenever one of their pupils finishes his studies and becomes properly educated or expert in the line of his education, in reality they share the happiness and moral pride with him. Humble Darvish teachers observe the living results of their own hard work, and thank God for the opportunity granted to them to be a positive part of this success.

To the heart and conscience of a truly humble and sincere teacher what can be more glorious and pleasant than the success of his Darvishes?

In Khaneghaah and by the teachings and guidance of his Master a Darvish learns that as a servant of true love he has no right to have any expectation, desire or passion for glory and pride. He is only a servant. Whatever service a Darvish may render to his society he must consider that opportunity as a blessing from Hagh and it is a serious responsibility to perform his duty properly to the highest possible level as is expected from responsible servants of LOVE and devotion.

A Darvish believes that whatever at a particular period of time he owns is granted to him with the responsibility to make the best use of that in the proper way. It is to be used for the benefit of others and for him as well. When the time comes and those properties or positions slip away, he is not to mourn. He remembers that the use of whatever he is losing is from now on designated to someone else who is also supposed to be responsible for that particular responsibility and duty until his time comes to an end; and the next after the other will face the same situation and cycle goes on; how can there be any cause for worry and grief?

Maktab e Tasavvof directs Darvishes involved in teaching and training others not only to understand their Darvishes in all sides and aspects of mentality, ability and psychology, but to feel and recognise their own situation, position and the consequent responsibilities from all aspects and to make the appropriate decision based on honesty and purity, sincerity and respect for everybody.

آموزش معلمی در آموزش به جامعه اش تعالیم پیامبران الهی را ماند در تعلیم
جامعه انسانی , مبارک , مقدس و ارزشمند و والامقام .

*"The teachings of a teacher to his society are like the
teaching of God's Prophets to the whole world; blessed,
holy valuable and prestigious."*

Hazrate Ghadeer Ali Shah

YOU ARE ALL FREE AND YOU ARE ALL RESPONSIBLE

A Darvish is a healthy and mature person; therefore he is similar to all other, intelligent, healthy and mature human beings. Not only does he enjoy all of the proper and constructive instincts, senses and feelings righteous people enjoy, he also may be tempted. A Darvish is equally susceptible to what is considered as faulty and destructive desires, passions and selfishness, as well as all of the other feelings human beings enjoy. This person always directly goes to solving the improper desire and never bends towards wrong. Based on all the training, guidance and spiritual direction a disciple receives in the Maktab, he will be alert for all the tricks and cheating, tricky thoughts and misguidance of his ego. Behaving responsibly, properly and with love for the whole of Creation he will investigate the situation, timing, condition, need, or whatever is attempting to divert and convert his thoughtful mind into an irresponsible one. The ego will not be capable and strong enough to change him towards the wrong and morally weak direction.

Sufism directs Darvishes to control their instincts and senses wisely using the knowledge held in their mind, the mind controlled and guided by the love radiated from their innocent and wise heart, the heart that is the temple of love, home for sincerity and place for corrections.

First and prior to any activity, Darvishes are to control and eliminate their own improper passion, desire, wants, demands and expectations, self-centering and acts of ego; the qualities that do not help to have a happy, worry-free and griefless life.

Sufism is a school where ordinary people are trained to become honoured servants of society; helping them to straighten their manners and behaviours to improve their relation with other people in private and socially. Sufism's teaching is to assist people to direct their thought in the right direction. This school also conducts them to proper and right methods to correct whatever is wrong inside and outside themselves (thoughts, ideas, action and behaviours). Sufism teaches and guides disciples to eliminate their rebellious desires, to develop proper and healthy thoughts and wishes for the benefit and good of the whole of Creation, as well as for themselves.

The above are only outward results of this Maktab. They are consequences of purity and honesty and sincerity. Remember, at the time a person surrenders to Hagh, he dies out of all imperfections and resurrects in the holiness of God.

We have to admit that many people find those corrections and eliminations are not so easy to achieve, and to reach the goals beyond those qualities are even harder; but to the people who have heartfelt intention even much higher goals than this are easily achievable. In all cases, in order to be capable to ascend to higher pure qualities and arrive at any position discussed above, what is vital is to eliminate improper habits, behaviours, actions and thoughts in their mind.

Darvishes are aware that it is not possible for an ordinary man to control all of his instincts, desires, wishes and ego in the short period of time following when he decides to do so. Darvishes have the understanding that such a great decision is not easily achievable, that the wish cannot take place overnight. Even with continuous and sincere endeavour, it will not happen without the person being under the protection, guidance, direction, and teaching of a true Master, and even so, it must have the blessing of Hagh bestowed on both the person's will, and his Master's, for the correction to take place. The Blessing will be granted and bestowed upon those people who prove their sincerity and truthfulness through long, permanent and continuous patience, continuous practices, obedience to love and keeping control of all decisions and thoughts under the guidance, wisdom and direction of feelings of their heart. Sufism works with the heart to control the mind.

All decisions should all be based and influenced by love and by the commands of the heart while the mind's knowledge, experience and subsequent suggestions are to be considered. It is the vital and the most important duty of the mind to help it's Master (Man) to make right and proper decisions to the benefit of everyone involved, particularly and protecting his master's own benefit. Hagh has given Man the brain and power to collect evidence, gather knowledge and from then on consider, think and decide, but regretfully the untamed and rebellious mind persuades it's Master to make the best benefit and use of everything for his own benefit no matter what the rights of the other parties involved are. Dishonest and selfish decisions made by a rebellious mind appear to be pleasant but sooner or later dishonesty will show

جمله معشوق است و عاشق پرده ای

its ugly face and the poor man, cheated by his mind, has to pay a huge price for that mistake.

Permanent happiness will not be achievable unless the mind is trained and convinced that only wise, true and constructive knowledge is held in the heart therefore consultation with, and then listening to, the wisdom of the heart is vital. The heart is the temple of love, chamber of sincerity, honesty and purity. It is through the light and guidance of love that honest, holy, and constructive decisions are made. The heart will consider and evaluate the material and spiritual consequences of any decision made on the life of people and their society. The heart does not make mistakes.

When you look around you and evaluate what people consider success or happiness, what do you discover? Are people truly tranquil? Don't you believe that it is the time for Man to wake up from his unachievable dreams and feel true life, true happiness, true tranquility and true success?

Man should understand that material pleasures, no matter how glorious and glamorous they appear to be, are short-lived, while the consequent grief and regrets left behind from improper and dishonest actions will last longer and potentially damage the person's present and future.

The heavy grief and burden of a guilty conscious does not easily leave the heart of the guilty person. A guilty person has to pay his penalty and receive and bear grief and bitterness for what he does exactly the same as an honest and sincere man who receives pleasure and happiness as a prize for his honest and sincere actions.

تاسف باد بر آنانی که دیانت حقه حضرت حق را در لذت از اجرای نیکی ها و تحری از پلیدی ها پاس نمیدارند

"Woe to the people who do not support the religion of Allah by enjoining GOOD and forbidding EVIL."

Hazrate Saadegh

جمله معشوق است و عاشق پرده ای

157

The person who gives preference to true simplicity and honesty over the false glory and position is a Darvish. Be a Darvish: be meek, be sincere, be honest, and be indigent. Find glory in simplicity and service—the pleasure in giving and happily rendering service is more pleasant than receiving it.

Wisdom is another great blessing bestowed and granted to Man so that he may carefully direct and control his mind and direct it to sincerely observe the material world to the best of its capacity, so that he will consider what is truly serious and important, so that nothing of importance and influence may be missed or ignored. At the time of decision-making it is wise and responsible to direct the mind to make appropriate decisions based on the results achieved from the mind's experiences, studies and knowledge.

In Khaneghaah the Darvishes are trained to remember that honesty, reality, truth, sincerity and perfection must come first. From the highest position, playing the original and principal role in the healthy and successful life of any society, the school of Sufism teaches the Darvishes that protecting and securing the demands of a material life has to have limits. To a degree, it is the people who, at the time of making a decision, should consider morality and honesty and place it above their personal materialistic wishes. The mind should be permitted on the basis of knowledge and experience to make decisions, but to make only honest and just decisions. It must consider the end result of those decisions. Wisdom suggests to an experienced and obedient mind to consider the rights of all of the other people or creatures involved and how they will be affected by the decision.

As soon as the mind goes astray and gives poor advice to the person and the consequent decision is made, then it is too late and the situation is unacceptable to a pure, sincere person. What or who should control the mind at this point of time and is the proper authority and/or power to prevent Man from making such a mistake? What else could it be except his Heart?

The heart is the land of truth and honesty, ascending high to the heavens of love and truthfulness, a different direction from ego and selfishness. It is up to the sincerity, honesty and integrity of any person, that when he is to make a decision, he gives the higher position to his heart and its recommendations. The uncontrolled mind is the seat of the devil (ego) for those people to whom honesty is not in their character. Those people get persuaded by their ego and passion and not by love and devotion and the results of all decisions are selfish.

جمله معشوق است و عاشق پرده ای

The heart purely directs Man to practice honesty, sincerity and to behave properly. Sufism teaches the disciples that all human beings are equal and deserve honesty and heartfelt feelings towards them, particularly those innocents, victims, sick people, and the needy, all because in the presence of Hagh they are all equal and hold equal position. The role and responsibility of the heart, the temple of Love and house of Hagh is to convince Man to perform his duties and do good things for everybody, to prepare a just, peaceful, honest and pure environment for all creatures, to make everyone honestly happy, even if it is in contrary to physical and material pleasure and benefit of himself. The person who listens to the advice of the holy and innocent heart is a Darvish.

The role of Sufism on any occasion is not to decide instead of the person himself, it is evident and clear that in reality Sufism cannot make this decision, but can direct him, advise him, persuade and assist him to make the right honest, pure, and proper decision based on Truth that is acceptable to all. This is HAGH—Right, True and Straight. The teachings of Sufism help Man to practice properly the right method for fair judgment, sincere service and honest actions. It teaches him to be responsible enough to control and overtake the ego's position and become master over his instincts; to do the right thing. However, if this person is under the control of a rebel mind which refuses to accept this suggestion, ignores directions from his heart, and decides to go astray then it is the person's fault. He is destroying his happiness with his own hands.

The decision maker is always the individual and that is where he has to use the benefit of the knowledge he has, and under the direction of heart's wisdom, make a wise and right decision. On the basis of this freedom to decide, he is fully responsible for his decisions and his actions in this material life on this planet. It should not be forgotten that Man's HELL or PARADISE is created and decided at this stage, and that, according to this freedom, Man is free to decide to act evil or truthfully, in the right or wrong way; Man is responsible and accountable for his actions and has to accept consequences.

Sufism teaches guides, directs and persuades Man to listen to his heart and give advantage to his heartfelt feelings and pure innocent emotions over the material thoughts and desires of his mind, ego and instincts. It is through the heart that a wise man feels responsible and considers life before making a decision. Such a decision is Hagh—true and right, as it is wisely and properly considered from all sides and dimensions.

جمله معشوق است و عاشق پرده ای

You are all FREE and you are all RESPONSIBLE

Qur'an

IN THE WORLD OF NO DESIRE, NO ONE IS POOR

A devoted Darvish is to see, observe, think wisely, compare and then decide if matters are beautiful or ugly, hard or easy, cheap or expensive, right to perform or if it is more wise and beneficial to ignore and forget about them. These comparisons and consequent decisions are heartfelt, spiritual, and sincere and beyond the material anxieties and wishes. For the person whose thoughts are desirous, greedy, and selfish and ruled by ego, a right and honest decision is a hard decision to make, even impossible. Under the teaching of Sufism when a Darvish decides to put his desires and ego aside and listens for truth and purity he will be capable of making the right decision.

Sufism teaches the disciples to have few materialistic desires and to not obey their ego, to step-by-step and case-by—case reduce any kind of expectation and have less demands or wishes for material objects which do not help them create an environment that is moral and humane. Sufism expects that the disciple grants and gives what he can and surrenders his complete existence to Hagh. The best a disciple may do is to render more and more service. This teaching can even bring materially successful results to the disciple while he is under the light of purity and gradually advancing on the path of Truth. Thus by the guidance of the Master, direction of The Path, and Blessing bestowed by Hagh, the disciple travels step-by-step out of his ego and moves towards purity. This teaching helps the disciple to know he is to serve, help, assist, give and offer his sincerity and heartfelt works with all of his honesty and ability in the field of his expertise to all who have needs to be served. Meanwhile, he will come to a point of humbleness and meekness with true human qualities, this is the breaking point between an ordinary worldly person and A Complete Man and it is now that the person, in his heart feels, that he himself has no right to expect his own glory and fame, is not allowed and permitted to demand, ask for, expect or even think of having anything in exchange for what he gives or offers.

At this stage the Darvish is so absorbed in the love of his beloved Hagh that nothing else can make him happy or cause him to become sad. The Darvish does not claim or wish for anything for himself. He controls his desires, has no selfish desires and no wishes for material goods. He practices sincerity, meekness, and love.

Maktab e Tasavvof is the school of true humanity, where people attend with the hope of learning the way of freely giving while they do not want or wish or expect to receive.

A Darvish is the one that to him, whatever social position and prestige he may enjoy, does not have any place in his heart, mind or dreams as a position of prestige. They are merely parts of the duty he is appointed to serve. Such a person is a truly rich, wealthy and happy creature in his heartfelt and spiritual life. He is not jealous, greedy, demanding and corrupt.

In the worldly and material life of today Man seriously is entangled in numerous desires, passions, expectations and hopes. Many people, instead of trying to get themselves out of their problems, do not stop. They cause more troubles for themselves by always dreaming of new wishes for any kind of thing, no matter if they have any use for them or not. Their mind and thoughts are so overloaded and busy that there is no time left for them to try to stop and observe, think and feel. They do not have time to consider that beyond all of the hassles exists something more important and valuable and indeed this lifestyle is simple, clean, neat, joyful and happy without any struggle. Man does not even dream that the purpose of his Creation and the life granted to him is much higher and purer than all of positions and conditions he wishes for or the troubles and difficulties he is experiencing in today life.

To a Sufi the real pleasure in life is from experiencing the true, innocent and pure feelings of his heart, in feelings of love, in sincere devotion, in humble morality and spirituality. Darvishes believe that when the heart acts only with those great qualities the consequent achievement will be the sincere, honest, heartfelt and pure thoughts. Those thoughts in their turn help the person to change any troubles and unhappy periods in his life into successful and happy ones, or at least view them in an acceptable, neutral and real way. Such a person will feel and understand true and real happiness the same as the happy man who had no shirt.

When a Darvish sees the unhappy life many people are experiencing and are struggling with he feels sorry for them, he has compassion for them and thinks how easy it would be for those troubled people to distance themselves from all

جمله معشوق است و عاشق پرده ای

of those difficulties. A Darvish believes that if those troubled people decided to change their present miserable condition with some heartfelt sincerity and effort they can be capable to change the misery. Some Darvishes, through their personal experiences, believe that if troubled people sincerely want to change, it may be fully and completely possible to be changed. A Darvish knows those people's miserable life can be changed and transferred into a relaxed, easy and griefless life. Their restless way of living may change into a glorious heavenly life only if they decide honestly to focus on a happy, pleasant and stress-free life. A life which does not need any more rushing, fighting, corruption, bribing or aggression or any of the actions some people perform to get material articles their mind thinks will bring the happiness.

A life glorified with love and beauty, purity and blessing, a truly happy and simple life is achievable for everyone provided they truly and sincerely wish to understand real happiness, no matter what position they may have. They will have it provided they can distinguish what a truly happy life is.

تـا ز حـس بیرون نیایـد آدمـسـی

So long as man doesn't come out of his material senses

بـاشـسـد از تصـویر غیبـی اعجمـی

Ignorant of transcendent entities he remained

Persian Poem

A really happy life will be achievable only on one very simple condition and that is, when people commit to having such a life. Humans are thoroughly created to have a life based on love, purity and simplicity. When they have this way of life they will admit that the new life of theirs is a life different from what they had in the past. The level of happiness is so enchanting that when they experience bright and happy conditions of their new life they will admit that in their previous life, in spite of all of their hard work, they were totally unable to dream of such a happy and relaxed life. Those people, in their former life were never able to think that they would taste this level of a pleasant griefless life. Those people, with their new type of life experience, when they think back how confusing their life in the past has been will be surprised. The way of thinking they used to have in the old days, what they aggressively wanted to possess e.g. a higher position, more luxury items, larger homes and bigger cars, it looks childish and funny. How wrongly they had thought that those items would bring them satisfaction and happiness; they will somehow be sad but also laugh at their life in those days, and clearly understand what a fantasy it has been.

New comers and disciples to the school of Sufism discover in their new plain and simple life that gradually, much to their surprise, the expensive luxury possessions and high positions they were wishing for in their previous life no longer have any value or interest for them. Their new life will be much simpler and more comfortable than the complicated and miserable life they used to have. Even though their wealth, position and possessions may not have changed, what has changed is the station of their soul and settlement of their mind. From this change of perspective everything else has changed accordingly.

The indigent, poor and meek Darvish begs people to create and maintain a happy simple and relaxed life for them, which in turn will change their environment and atmosphere for everyone else.

Sufism trains the Darvish to direct himself into a real and true life and to avoid being caught in the illusions and dreams of an unclear future. This school trains the disciple to open his sensible and sincere eyes and see life's reality then has him touch reality, taste reality, and feel the absolute reality of his own life in his heart. Through experience a Darvish feels how easily a simple and humble life is. The Darvish then opens his eyes and heart to see the real beauty and understands that throwing out of his mind all of the rebellious, greedy and terrible dreams is both simple and practical. All of these wonderful experiences are possible and achievable if he is determined to surrender to LOVE's sincerity and simplicity.

According to the teachings of this school in the heart is where true feelings are both felt and enjoyed. That means love and real happiness grows continually inside the heart, this repository of fidelity, obedience and simplicity in life. It is from this great treasure that the perfume of pleasure and happiness spreads to the whole environment. Maktab Darvish—The school of Darvish-hood continually reminds

جمله معشوق است و عاشق پرده ای

him that there is nothing outside him which may create or bring happiness or even sadness and grief to him; it is all inside his heart and in obedient to his mind.

A simple life and plain life but with deep roots in love and devotion; this is the life of Man when he has firm control over his instincts, desires and expectations.

در دل بی آرزو راه غم و تشویش نیست

In an entirely desire-less heart no worry or woe

در جهان بی نیازی هیچ کس درویش نیست

In the world of having no desire, none is poor

Persian poem

جمله معشوق است و عاشق پرده ای

YOU ARE BLESSED WITH WHAT YOU ARE,

NOT WITH WHAT YOU HAVE

To an ordinary materialistic person being content, humble and in control of excessive desires, being able to sacrifice the wishes of passion and the will of the physical body seems to be hard, in fact impossible. When this person brings his instincts under the supervision of the wisdom of his heart and tames his mind with right knowledge it will not be impossible anymore.

A Sufi as is not expecting to get any satisfaction or happiness from other people's recognition of his social and spiritual condition. A Darvish does not show off whom or what he is. He is simple and just considers himself as a simple, plain, ordinary person and far from glory. A Darvish is to live simply, direct his life simply, work simply, serve simply, and feel simply, as any ordinary indigent man has to live. This is the life of a Darvish and it is the same as the time he was born, when he was nobody and had nothing, helpless and powerless at the mercy of the midwife.

There are people who are unable to control their instincts, ego, pride, and self-centering. These people believe that they are the most important, superior, or most holy of holies, most spiritual, never making any mistakes; their education, knowledge, understanding and fame are beyond the whole of Creation, those we should call sick minded people. Those poor people are far from the teachings and expectations of this school, or any school of dignity and humbleness. How can those type of people claim to be indigent, meek, poor or a Darvish? It is a moral question for them to answer, they are the poor sick people who need to repent, apologise and beg for forgiveness for their mistaken thinking.

A Darvish, through the teachings and directions of his Master and in the environment of Khaneghaah, learns not to forget that all human beings at the time of their birth are born, poor, naked, helpless and indigent. They, all of them, are at the mercy and in the palm of the hand of the mid-wife and beyond that at the mercy of their Destiny.

جمله معشوق است و عاشق پرده ای

As importantly the Sufi, in the course of his training, is reminded that he must never forget the vital and important last moment, the moment he has to leave this world again; again he is naked, poor indigent and at the mercy of undertakers.

نـــــــه بر اشـــتری ســوارم

I am neither mounted on a camel,

نـــــو چـــــو خـر به زیر بارم

nor loaded on as a donkey

نـــه خداوند رعیــــت

I am neither lord of any subjects,

نـــه غـــــلام پادشاهم

nor slave of his Majesty

Persian Poem

Man comes to this material world naked and poor and he leaves this material world poor and naked. He materially brings nothing to this world and materially takes nothing out of it either.

A Master teaches the disciples what the vital facts of life are. A whole program of the school is to help disciples understand that life is plain, simple, easy and comfortable. The person who feels or thinks differently must look for the cause or reason inside his mind and its desires. The school directs the Darvishes to incline and concentrate their heart's feelings as well as the attention of their mind towards the simplicity and beauty of life. As they are trained Darvishes are expected to manage their lives according to the simple fact that will direct them towards the path of contentment:

YOU ARE BLESSED WITH WHAT YOU ARE, NOT WITH WHAT YOU HAVE

In the light that Molana Rumi, a great mystic poet and a simple Darvish a great mystic poet and a simple Darvish confesses his 'I' is nothing, he is nobody, and his physical existence and the wealth is less than nothing then how can other people submersed in their ego and selfishness claim to be the greatest of the great and centre for everything?

جمله معشوق است و عاشق پرده ای

ESSENCE IS FROM THE ONE, THOUSANDS ARE FACES

Based on the teachings of sincerity, honesty, meekness and purity, which a Darvish receives he is seriously expected to believe the fact that ignorance is the greatest poison that affects humanity.

Sufism is for all Mankind who intend to walk in this direction: all humans from any colour, nationality, belief, religion, education, creed, sect, and whatever system of living and condition they may practice. Sufism is a path and school where truth, happiness and simplicity are not limited to a group of people; it belongs to all and every creature. It is up to them to get close and pick the colourful, aromatic and soft rose of happiness.

When a man believes he is simply a person who is similar to his neighbour and the neighbour of his neighbour that is the time he is ready to serve and expect no reward, ready to give and not hope to receive in exchange. Such a person is a Sufi, a Darvish, and he has a plain but happy life.

Sufism embraces all humans who wish to join this school, attend its teachings and follow its directions and also for those who are interested in simplicity and sincerity. The gates of this Maktab are wide open to all of those who wish to become servants for the whole of Creation in general and humanity in particular. Sufism's goal, aim and hope are to persuade all of Mankind to adore, admire and respect humanity and accept their fellow humans as Caliphs and representatives of Hagh on earth.

ای فرزند , بدان که به واقع , آدمی بود هیچی است در میان دو هیچ

O' my son be aware that in reality MAN is a nothing in between two nothings.

Abbas Ali Shah, a Darvish Master – from Isfahan

جمله معشوق است و عاشق پرده ای

Sheykh Mahmood e Shabesatari in his famous book—Golshane Raaz (The Flower Garden of Secrets)—has a verse, which may be interpreted as, Hagh is one, His people are numerous, but they all are reflections of His light.

یک وجود آمد ولی صورت هزار

All Mankind are the same only different in their appearance.

کثرت صورت ندارد اعتبار

Essence is from the One, thousands are faces

The credit is not in those many faces.

Sheykh Mahmood e ShabesatariGolshane Raaz

(The Flower Garden of Secrets)

Sheykh Mahmoud, in this very influential verse, describes to Mankind a very vital and important fact which reminds them to be humble and recognise where the seat of their real, proper position and place in this world is located.

The real value of a human is not considered and measured by his physical weight, physical appearance, colour, race, sect, nationality, religion or amount of education and money he possesses and not even the number of his employees and his position or external appearance. The value of a man is in the way and the method he appreciates and values his true position in the path to Hagh—The Absolute Truth—and its consequence in his heartfelt services. Feelings, manners, and love for all Creation; this is the foundation, source, and place of Sufism ethics.

جمله معشوق است و عاشق پرده ای

PREVENTION IS MORE EFFECTIVE, FASTER, POSSIBLE AND EASIER THAN TO TRY THAN FINDING A CURE

A Sufi is the person whose life is based on his acknowledgment of his true position in life, understands what he truly owns, appreciates the level of responsibility he has and properly performs his duties towards the whole of Creation as an act of devotion to Hagh. He believes he is nothing, owns nothing and possesses nothing; he acts as a tool, with no more importance than any other tool. His duty is to do his best, to put his best effort in the performance of his job, use his ability and wealth to help and complete other human's lives so that they may have a safe, just, happy and sound life. When a tool is imperfect and unable to perform the job it is supposed to then what is the use of it? The same is an imperfect person who is an imperfect tool, or improper for the job he is expected to accomplish. The school of Sufism is eagerly prepared and ready to teach and train any person who is interested and willing to be generous, nice, kind, logical, honest and sympathetic to others, because a Darvish believes that in fact these qualities are already bestowed on every human being, only the person must decide to promote and let them grow, flourish and blossom.

Sufism directs Mankind to have heartfelt feeling towards ALL and as such, insists that people creatively finds proper solutions to the daily problems in life. This help could be for themselves, other people and even animals, plants, birds, waters, mountains, or space. Everything in the whole world is created by Hagh and a Darvish is a person to serve ALL to the best of his ability and capacity. A Sufi must make all of his decisions for Hagh and believe that any decision made with love and harmony will make life happy and will save Man from the miserable and terrifying problems he is facing in the materialistic system of modern life. The solution to help Mankind is the sincere, pure and simple way of life, based on heartfelt decisions and the wisdom and proper thinking. Prevention is more effective, faster, possible and easier to try, than a cure.

Khaneghaah is the home where the gates are always wide open to everybody, no matter whether they are a Darvish or not, believer or atheist, educated or uneducated, rich or poor, human or just a living creature. The main and most vital responsibility and duty of Khaneghaah is to help the needy in any field (up to its capacity and ability). Khaneghaah has to help, direct and guide anybody who has an intention to get more information about Darvish-hood or Sufism. It is responsibility of the Sheykh of the Khaneghaah to assist the person who wishes to brighten his life with love, devotion, positive and constructive hopes, with both happiness and with pleasure.

- ❖ Do Sufis and Darvishes make miracles?

- ❖ Do they perform the impossible?

- ❖ And is what the Darvishes create admirable?

Of course Darvishes make miracles, but not the kind of miracle either ordinary and simple people or greedy and materially thinking people expect. Darvishes do not perform material magic, but they pour LOVE out of their heart, mind, mouth, eyes and through their actions to wherever, whenever and whoever needs it. They bring LOVE to the people, offering LOVE to everyone. Darvishes, by speaking and by the way they listen, through sincere attention, by their stories and explanation of problems, miraculously show their love. By their hands and feet Darvishes' offer Love when at the service of those people. Darvishes make their miracles when they pour their sincerity over the other people's needs, all of that is their magic and their miracle. A Darvish's LOVE is the greatest magic and the only magic such a meek and indigent person performs.

The next miracle of Sufism is to persuade people to look into their own heart and to listen to the holy wishes of its call and to the direction it directs them to. Darvishes lovingly beg people to permit the flow of love pour out of their hearts to all Creation and thus relieve them from misery; the misery both they and their society are experiencing. When this message and miracle of Sufism is well heard and performed the society becomes treated and purified. It is expected from such a pure and proper society that the society in its turn will offer and give to its members a life that is continuously relaxed and happy, with comfort and satisfaction.

جمله معشوق است و عاشق پرده ای

اگر در آئی در باز است و اگر نیایی خدای بی نیاز است.

If you wish to enter the gates of Beneficence and Mercy are
wide open, but if you deny God is not in indigence He needs
not

Persian maxim

TRUTHFULLY THE TRUE OWNER IS GOD

Many mental, emotional, material, and financial problems the Man of today is facing are caused and created from one source, only one factor; their unrealistic desires. Particularly in the case where they are not certain if they may achieve what their desires and their passion expect to achieve. When a person is not tranquil in his heart and his mind, he will never feel happy and comfortable. Such person is always worried and tense unless he succeeds to satisfy his greedy and tempting mind, making that mind happy by feeding what it demands. The demands are worldly, material and unnecessary, merely ornaments, and providing a false sense of security. The person has no security in his mind as compensation and merely wishes for more personal power on one hand and more respect from the society on the other. This person expects his society to make everything perfect and glorious for him, but he himself? He never bothers to think if he deserves what he wants and wishes!

The Man of today never stops greedily and selfishly wishing and wanting. The desires are his greatest problem, the problems that never will be solved. Because this demanding person never stops; in his unsettled mind he never feels secure, will always be insecure and at the end of his life has unsolvable problems, not because there is not a solution for it but because he created it that way.

A Darvish is happy with what he has, with all that he receives and with all he earns through sincere and honest hard work. He does not put all of his hopes, wishes and efforts on securing his financial matters or social position. He gives priority to real and positive matters in life such as being a better person in his society, to be a more active servant at the service of his beloved Hagh. To be a meek person, an honest and simple person, a happy and serving person, he performs his duties and leads his life exactly as a person in love. He does not want anything for his own, but for the happiness and satisfaction of his beloved.

Let us go back to our talks, and speak about the occasions when people face grief, sadness, get depression, and even contemplate suicide.

جمله معشوق است و عاشق پرده ای

When a person is expected to do a favour for another person, no matter if this second person is a close relation or a stranger, when the person depended on is not capable to perform the expected favour, he becomes angry, hostile, disappointed with the person asking the favour but also sad and unhappy inside himself. Why?

Maybe the nature of demand was outside of his ability. Perhaps he knows that he cannot satisfy the person's wishes. It may well be impossible RIGHT NOW to do what is being asked. But rather than look respectfully at his own capacity to fulfill the request he not only does not accept his own explanation and becomes angry, hostile and disappointed with the person requesting the favour but also feels disappointed, sad and unhappy inside himself.

Lots of psychological problems, physical illnesses, the many restless and uncomfortable nights tossing and turning, the addictions to drugs or alcohol, car accidents, mistakes at work and thousands of other unpleasant and unexpected matters in life are reactions and consequences have their root in that one desire to please someone else. Is it that important? Is it worth all of the pain?

Those unrealistic expectations and thoughts disturb the mind with such unrealistic goals that consequently through ugly thoughts, hatred, disappointment, and grief turns the life of a person from a bright and happy spring day into a miserable dark, long and cold winter night. Why should this happen to anyone?

There are many other difficulties and problems that exist; they are easily brought to mind. In Sufism the solution for those problems is quite simple:

BE HAPPY

Simple and easy to understand advice:

- ❖ Be happy with what you have in hand and work happily for what you logically hope to achieve by your sincere attempts and honest hard working, definitely you will receive what you truly deserve.

- ❖ Expect only what you deserve, not what your ego dictates.

- ❖ Be sure that the real positive and constructive necessities of life will be supplied as they are achievable. Simple, proper and relevant wishes will be granted and blessed. Your needs will be provided for if they are right, logical and for the good of everyone.

The school of Sufism advises Darvishes to be aware of the tricks of mind which persuade the person to chase the desires of his dreams, the tricks which will turn the Darvishes away from their true duties, feelings and sentiments.

The heart says: You are at the service of all creatures and everyone; while the untamed mind says: Everyone is at your service and for your comfort.

And a Darvish is slave of love, obedient to the direction, guidance and commands of his heart which directs him to sincerity, honesty and true love and advises him to:

❖ Be charitable and generous to needy, to those people who are less fortunate than you.

❖ Be passionately a true lover of Creation.

❖ Be wise and do not deny and curse the world. Do not forget that this world in which you live in is a truly beautiful Creation

❖ Understand the world properly and appreciate that surely not only does the world similarly understand you, but in fact gives you a lot of valuable experiences freely.

❖ Curse any greedy, egoistic, self-centering and destructive passions which are residing in your mind. Remember that they are the ones to be controlled and tamed.

❖ Always remember that it is this world which is producing your needs, therefore in exchange it is your duty to work for its purity and progress.

❖ Be thoughtful of the fact that whatever wealth you have at your possession is granted to you for your comfort but in the meantime you are responsible and are expected morally to share the benefits with others.

جمله معشوق است و عاشق پرده ای

- ❖ Fairness, equality and justice hold the greatest position for the security of the life of each and every individual and society of Mankind on Earth. Do not forget you are merely one individual out of all of those people.

Truck drivers spend most of their time, day and night, on the road with little time at home. Those drivers are generally plain, simple and sincere people, their feelings simple, and their love real and pure; they have sympathetic feeling for everything and everyone. These drivers in the day and night drive their heavy trucks for very long distances. They have a very particular lifestyle, physically rough while soft and romantic inside. At night they drive under the deep blue and star filled sky of their country, across the beautiful and colourful mountains, illuminated by the silver light of moon. While driving in the daytime they enjoy the vast panoramic views of coast, plains and colourful valleys.

In Iran, while driving, they usually listen to simple folk music commonly composed on the famous meaningful Persian folk poems. Some of those drivers even go further and hire artists to paint some representative scenes or have calligraphy, writing some of those poems or idioms either on the rear parts of their trucks or on the top of the front part of their vehicles. The poems or idioms are mostly simple but meaningful and easy to understand. One of the poems which is commonly written trucks reads as under:

در حقیقت مالک اصلی خدا است

Truthfully the true owner is God

بهر روزی این امانت نزد ما است

This is granted to us to secure our daily sustenance

A Persian proverb

جمله معشوق است و عاشق پرده ای

The above poem and the intention of the person who chooses to have it written on his truck are representing emotions, thoughts, way of life, beliefs, desires, and the mentality of the person. The poems or idioms represent and introduce great meaning which in its turn deeply influences the people's thoughts with a message so deep in meaning yet connected directly to the daily life of everyone. The message travels all around the country, distributing the great meaningful message of meekness, innocence and happiness to everyone and everybody. Those messages can brighten the lives of people provided they stop for a moment, read the message of the poem, consider and act with the intention.

Across the world drivers are mostly simple, open, generous, not desiring much, not casting the power of their egoistic demands on anything or anyone. In fact they live and lead a Darvish life, but they do not carry a title with them. "What is in a name?" as Shakespeare wrote.

A true Darvish practices this simplicity in his daily life; he simply gives, and offers without showing off or expecting any kind of reward and/or praise for him. A Darvish, for his services, wants nothing in return since he knows his life is a temporary blessing bestowed upon him, his duty is to love and show his devotion. A Sufi who is here in this world now and has the opportunity to serve today serves, and enjoys seizing the positive opportunity since he does not know what tomorrow is going to bring.

When a Darvish practices and completes the exercises that his Master teaches him most of the problems that once in the past appeared to be fierce and life threatening will turn out to be tamed and bearable. Through the lessons he knows that there will be an end to each and every one of those hard and difficult conditions and unpleasant times, while the spiritual experiences and the precious and valuable achievements will stay with him forever.

Any intelligent person admits that the end of the material life of all humans is the same, they all finally will die, be poor, helpless, and naked in the hands of undertakers. The part of the person which will not end with death, which remains in this material world after death is the good or bad reputation—the measure of the intention and the love held in the heart, which transcends all worldly matters.

Love, sincerity, helping others and good intention are the true higher values and remain in this world long after death. Darvishes certainly aim to leave the legacy

جمله معشوق است و عاشق پرده ای

of a good reputation but more than this they believe that life continues after death and the consequences of any action, no matter good or bad, will stay with them and affect their afterlife.

A Darvish looks at the world and its worldly possessions with a much less complicated view than most people make in their own life. A Darvish looks at life without material desires, wishes or greed. The Darvish observes life peacefully, a much different opinion from those who cast their hopes, wishes and desires upon the material part of life. From the Darvish's point of view those people make their life harder and harder, they enjoy less and suffer more. Darvishes believe:

A wise person never wants to suffer.

When a Darvish looks at those people who make their own life difficult and full of misery, empty of any hope and happiness, so difficult and unbearable, they wonder at how this person of so much confusion can be of any service or help to their society.

Then the Darvish, as a morally responsible member of the human family, observes the situation finds the problems, gets involved in helping them, and assists the confused person to make their lives easier and more comfortable. This Darvish wants nothing for himself in this treatment and solution. This Darvish's ego lacks a strong grip on him because the holy feelings of his heart are in command. Those pure and innocent feelings and their consequent thought are in control of his ego. His existence is top-to-toe love and devotion. He wishes all the good and all the happiness for every other creature created by his Beloved. In his heart he knows the true love of Hagh created everything and everyone and so all of them deserve his sincere and lovingly free service.

To a Darvish as his first service is to provide comfort and happiness for others. His hope is to assist, direct and help them to understand true and real happiness. This is not the happiness which is thought to exist in material properties, but the true heartfelt love and happiness of having a controlled and tamed ego. He wants every man to know when ego is controlled and the destructive passions are tamed, selfishness and egoistic desires have no place in the life of the person and as a result naturally a lot of daily troubles are erased and life becomes less hectic and difficult.

I HAVE CREATED MAN FROM CLAY AND I HAVE
BLOWN FROM MY SPIRIT IN HIM

In the first stage Sufi Masters guide the Darvishes to understand the real productive ambition for life, to recognise what the constructive desires are, and what is proper and honest work and what should be considered as proper constructive and positive competition. They guide and show the Darvishes a simple way to achieve the higher human goals, the achievements which are well blessed and admired. Those teachings and exercises are the means by which a person may travel to the destination of purity, humbleness and selflessness.

سـعدی یا دی رفت و فردا همچنـان خواهد گذشت

O Saadi, yesterday is passed, and similarly will tomorrow

د ر مـسیان این و آن فرصت شمـا ر امـروز را

Seize opportunity of today in between of the two

Saadi the great Poet from Shiraz

The Darvish is assisted and directed by his Master to investigate, study and judge his own thoughts, desires, wishes and actions very hard and very accurately. He also learns how to not judge but to observe and see the cause beneath some people's passion and desires and their consequent actions, to consider if they are positive or negative, constructive and/or destructive. The Master teaches the Darvish to think about the main reason behind the instincts bestowed on Man. The positive, constructive and blessed wishes or passions he has or should have for

جمله معشوق است و عاشق پرده ای

life matters. The Master describes to the Darvish all of the sincere, positive and constructive feelings within him are blessings bestowed upon him. They are to be utilized so that he may take benefit from and make himself thrive.

Man is equipped with desires and instincts of ambition and competition so that he actively gets himself involved in making the life in his society more positive, better, safer, easier, and constructive. This will make Man eager and interested in more knowledge, experience and expertise. This shows how a peaceful, friendly and loving society makes the life of its members happier, safer and more enjoyable. Man creates new inventions, finding easier methods for work. Ambition and competition assists him to study and search further in nature and Creation, to be more efficient and productive. To gain a proper understanding of the instincts helps everyone to be prepared to grant more and expect less, not to be jealous, aggressive, selfish, corrupt and stupid. Beauty, comfort, tasty and healthy foods are all created by those who have desire for a better and happier life and instincts are bestowed on Man to see those beauties and comforts, feel them and enjoy from them, but up to a proper point and degree. Those are all means and not aims; they are all to give people the opportunity to find time to gain more education, experience and wisdom and to advance to better conditions.

> ملک دنیا تن پرستان را حلال
>
> For indulgent is the kingdom of this world
>
> ما غلام ملک عشق بی زوال
>
> For us is to be slaves to eternal love
>
> Moulana Rumi

In the teachings of the Sufism school none of the honest and productive attempts and activities of Man towards the direction of advancement physically, morally and spiritually, the service and help to Creation is condemned, but on the contrary is blessed, admired and praised.

جمله معشوق است و عاشق پرده ای

God Almighty, Merciful and Beneficent, says:

I have created man from Clay, and I have blown from MY SPIRIT in him

Quran, Chapter 15, verse 29

ALSO, in the LORD'S PRAYER Jesus Christ teaches to start our prayer as such:

O' OUR FATHER who art in heaven . . . .

This means that everybody and every person is a child of God and He is the father. Every person is bestowed with God's spirit. Every person has to respect himself as one who has been so loved and honoured by Hazrate Hagh, that they have been bestowed with holiness, glory, love, and blessings; to be a human being is to be a creative force.

Sufis see everything and everyone as representative of his Beloved Hagh on the Earth. Blessed with this understanding a Darvish respects, loves, serves, and sacrifices his own comfort in order to secure a successful and happy life, of course according to his ability and capacity, for Hagh's creation.

How can he not love everyone?

How can a Darvish dislike anyone?

How can a Darvish reject anybody? How can a day be in the life of a Sufi without shining his love and devotion towards others? A Darvish loves everyone and everything.

جمال ا وست هر جا جلوه کرد ه

It's His beauty which lusters through everywhere,

ز معشــوقان عــالم بسـته پر د ه

It lusters through the sweethearts of the world.

Persian poem

جمله معشوق است و عاشق پرده ای

A HEALTHY PERSON DOES NOT

NEED TO BE HOSPITALISED

What a devoted and sincere Darvish condemns:

- Greed

- Selfishness

- Self-centring

- Aggression

- Rejecting others

- Disrespecting others

- Picking on other people

- Gossiping about and slandering other people

Whoever is sick and affected by any one of the above sicknesses is a victim according to the guidelines and teachings of Khaneghaah. Such unhealthy and sick people need help and attention and are not to be rejected and scolded. The Darvish is responsible to find the right medicine to cure his sickness, to draw the evil thoughts out of the mind of this person. It is evident that the more sick and unconscious a patient is, the more he requires nursing, attention and more services. A healthy person does not need to be hospitalised, but a sick person does.

Sufism is the hospital for those sick people who need nursing and proper medical service to assist them until they are fully cured and become healthy again. Nobody is born with bad, incorrect and condemnable habits and thoughts, it is the life and the circumstances which caused those victims to be affected by the sicknesses they are suffering, they may be cured, and in fact it is their right to be cured. Their medicine is heartfelt LOVE and the treatment needs time and patience.

A Darvish pours the medicine of LOVE all over his sick patient and has to have plenty of time and patience to serve such a poor sick person.

Sufism is the school to train and educate people to advance to higher levels of humanity, to render services, and to observe human society as a uniquely, respectable body. This mission is not an impossible mission; it is a mission full of joy and happiness for the person who serves.

Jesus said:

Giving is more blessed than receiving

A Darvish is taught how to get out of ego and rid himself of the behaviours which make an ordinary person reject a sick person. A Darvish must get out of his bad manners, thoughts, and behaviour as a bird does get out of his eggshell. Both are being held back from growing and becoming complete and mature, to grow freely and properly.

WHY BE AFRAID?

A Sufi's service and devotion is unconditional.

A Darvish loves all creatures in Creation, but he does not expect a palace in Allah's paradise in exchange. He loves all and serves all with love. He lives in love. This love is not to gain him a favour from Hagh or because he wishes to be saved from the burning fire in Hell as an exchange for his sincere service.

A true lover loves his Beloved only because he loves her; if he has any expectation to receive anything from her in exchange for his love then he is a simple worker, expecting a salary, a worthless creature, not a true lover. A Darvish serves Creation because he is in love with his Creator, not to deserve paradise or because he has a fear of hell.

A Darvish, when it comes to his expectation from Hagh, is an extravagant and ambitious person, leaving praise or punishment for those people who are materially minded. He is not afraid of hell as he believes Hagh never tortures his Beloved creatures. Why be afraid?

Conversely a Darvish does not hope for Paradise, as he believes that Paradise is everywhere; it has no gates or walls. A true Darvish believes that it is stupid to desire what is given to everyone freely and with love.

The Darvish's wish from Hagh is Hagh, and nothing less. He does not have any transient, materialistic wish. But he must strive hard because he cannot expect Hagh for nothing; a lazy person does not receive the highest reward. To act the way Hagh wants a Darvish to act means that he has to sacrifice his entire existence and work with all of his heart and mind in His way. Through his actions, not his words and intentions, he must prove that he is a simple ray from Hagh's light in this world.

As a rose will spread its perfume without any hope for recognition, a Darvish will sincerely do his best, anonymously and humbly.

جمله معشوق است و عاشق پرده ای

WHAT EXISTENCE MAY A DARVISH HAVE?

The meaning of the word Darvish in Persian language—where the school has been founded and developed—is: meek, poor and indigent, own nothing, wish for nothing, and want for nothing. Based on these high foundations what existence may a Darvish have? Or what desire or wish may he have for material comforts?

There is one old Sufi parable:

> Once somebody asked a Sufi: what is your wish?

> In reply the meek Darvish said; I wish not to wish

A Darvish is God's creature, who has nothing, wants nothing, expects nothing, and in any respect needs nothing. He believes that he was created by Hagh through love, not in sin, and is granted everything he needs or has to have. He is a creature who until the last day in his life on the planet of earth loves, gives, devotes and serves.

Similar to everyone else he has got his life free. It is the knowledge of this that causes him to radiate free love everywhere and to everyone. What else does he need, what else can be so precious to him?

He believes that before he was created he was crowned with all the pride, glory and honour he was supposed to have. He believes that Hagh's blessings have been bestowed on all humanity as well. It is his intention then to make everyone aware and to show their appreciation and devotion to Hagh. A Darvish cannot oblige other people to admit and appreciate Divine love; he only can make them aware. It is, of course, up to them to respect, honour and to show their appreciation to Hagh.

جمله معشوق است و عاشق پرده ای

> آینه چون نقش تو بنمود راست
>
> When the mirror reflects your image truthfully
>
> خود شکن آئینه شکستن خطا است
>
> blame yourself, breaking the mirror is wrong
>
> Persian mystic poem

All he wishes for is happiness and comfort for other people to make their lives easier more comfortable, and to increase their real and true happiness. To him, a happy life is a life in a happy environment, thus he believes that his duty is to create the happy environment for the residents in his neighborhood so that each and every one of them enjoys life from a just, safe, happy and pure society.

> رسد آدمی به جائی که بجز خدا نبیند
>
> Man arrives to a position where from sees none but Allah
>
> بنگر که تا چه حد است مکان آدمیت
>
> Look how high is the position of man
>
> Persian Poem

Khajeh Abdollah one of most famous Darvishes ever known wrote books which offered guidance to followers of the teachings of the Path to lead them to the presence of their most beloved One, Hagh.

جمله معشوق است و عاشق پرده ای

بدان که ایمان بر سه وجه است که بیم و امید و مهر. بیم چنان میباید که تو را از
معصیت باز دارد و امید چنان میباید که ترا بر طاعت دارد و مهر چنان می
باید که در دل تو تخم خدمت کارد.

Be aware that faith consists of three dimensions which are
Fear, Hope, Love and affection.

Fear should be as such that prevents you from sins.

And Hope as such that persuade you in obedience and
devotion.

And affection as such which sow the seeds of service in your
heart.

KhaajehAbdollah

❖ A Sufi or Darvish does not, cannot and should not deceive people.

اگر درویش از الله جز الله خواهد در اجابت بر وی بسته شود.

If the Darvish asks Allah for anything but Allah,

the gates of acceptance will be closed to him.

KhaajehAbdollah"Maghoolaat"

❖ Darvishes should have simple and ordinary clothing to the standard
of their area, and suitable for their environment therefore, a Darvish
does not make any strange appearance for himself, does not wear
unusual clothing that is different from that which is acceptable and
is the custom of the society he lives in. Those who wear unusual
and strange clothing of any kind are the people who do not have

جمله معشوق است و عاشق پرده ای

confidence in their own abilities and are worried the society will find fault and weakness in them. A Darvish dresses, neat, clean, proper, respectable, cheap in price but expensive in value.

❖ A Darvish involves himself in respectable, positive, productive and social serving job or business. A devoted person never depends on other people to prepare and supply his needs, he is not a beggar. A Darvish is not a cheat, or lazy, and looking for his personal comfort and pleasure. He must be active productive and positively serve and do his society.

❖ Darvishes are expected to help the poor and disadvantaged people, such as those who are lonely, victims of bad luck and natural disasters, those who are victims of their society's immorality, the people who have been misused by other members in their society and when they have been of no more use to the users have been left helpless and without any shelter. When a person looks around he will see numerous examples of those unfortunate people.

❖ When a Darvish gets the opportunity to serve a person who is damaged in any respect e.g. rejected by his society, in need of moral, psychological, financial or medical support, the Darvish appreciates the opportunity and renders his service with utmost pleasure. Darvishes have to serve, all Mankind, animals, vegetation, anything in this Creation with best of their ability and possibility. A Darvish's service is for all and every one of Hagh—God—Allah—creatures, anyone and everyone, rich and poor, black and yellow, red and white, educated and peasant, great and small, intelligent and naive. A Darvish only sees the person not the personality.

❖ A Darvish must not get involved with intoxicants. Addiction to any kind of drug or intoxicating material is one of the most dangerous enemies of humanity. A Darvish has no permission to use or consume any quality, kind or type of narcotic. Sufism rejects any kind of intoxicant. Darvishes depend on Hagh and their own power and ability bestowed on them by Him, and not false and dangerous narcotics. The only addiction which a Darvish loves to be addicted to and is allowed to be addicted to is SERVICE, SERVICE and the SERVICE.

جمله معشوق است و عاشق پرده ای

- ❖ To a Darvish any duty designated for him is an important duty since he believes that it is designated by Hagh for his progress in his belief, his test, trial and making him ready for further progress.

- ❖ A Darvish is not corrupted or corrupts. He is guided to honesty and he is acting for the promotion and advancement of honesty. A Darvish rejects, refuses, and within his ability and power demolishes any improper and dishonest action and behaviour by other members of his society, not by fighting but with proper LOVE and GUIDANCE.

- ❖ A Darvish is not greedy as he believes what is designated for him or designated for anybody will be received in the right time. Therefore, a Darvish is not jealous, corrupted, dishonest, or expecting anything which is not honestly his and does not belong to him morally.

- ❖ A Darvish believes that he has no right to be annoyed or permission to annoy anyone. A Darvish believes improper action is one of the greatest sins committed.

- ❖ From a Sufi point of view and to Darvishes and/or Sufis all of those positions or possessions are considered as tools and means for the service and to serve others whom they are meant to serve. They are not the goal of Creation, merely tools for a productive life.

گـر پـارچـه گلیـم یـا کـه دیبـا است

No matter if the cloth is from rug or silk

چـون پـاک و تمیـز بود زیبـا اسـت

It is beautiful when neat and clean.

Saadi the Great Persian poet

جمله معشوق است و عاشق پرده ای

Monaajaat Naameh

Fervent Prayer To Oneness

حضرت خواجه عبد الله انصاری در مناجات نامه خویش بر درگاه حضرت
احدیت چنین می سراید که:

الهی تو آنی که از بنده نا سزا بینی و به عقوبت نشتابی . از بنده کفر می شنوی و
نعمت از او باز نگیری و توبت و انابت بر او عرضه کنی و به پیغام و خطاب
خود او را باز خوانی و اگر باز آمد او را و عده مغفرت دهی . پس چون با دشمن
بد کردار چنینی با دوستان نیکو کار چونی؟

*O' Lord – Ellahi – Thou art the one who sees His creatures
incompetent, and wicked, but Thou do not hasten to remunerate.*

*Hears blasphemy from slave but does not requisite His favour from
him but guide him to repentance.*

*Thou call him back through messages and when he returns grant him
Thy mercy and forgiveness.*

*Thou deal thus with such indecent mannered what will be Thy action
to obedient well behaved friends?*

KhaajehAbdollah"Monaajaat Naameh"

جمله معشوق است و عاشق پرده ای

THERE IS NO MATERIAL PRICE

Saadi, the great mystic wise man of several centuries ago in one of his poems describes a story:

One of the Sufi Masters was travelling in the desert and on his way he came across a dog. The poor dog was thirsty and close to death as there was no water within the dog's reach and no one to help the poor creature.

Without a second thought the Master immediately made a pot with his Darvishes' hat (Taaj) and a rope with his shawl, to pull water from a well in the area and put the water in his hat in front of the thirsty dog.

> خواجه عبد الله در رساله واردات بر سبیل پند و اندرز فرماید:
>
> اگر بر هوا پری مگسی باشی و اگر بر روی آب روی خسی باشی . دلی بدست آر تا کسی باشی.
>
> *If you fly in the air you are as a fly is, and if you walk on the water you will be as a mote is. Gratify one and you will be somebody.*
>
> Khaajeh Abdollah in epistle Vaaredaat "Incomings"

There is no material price that you can you can put on such an action. The poor dog does not know all the effort that has occurred and what that man has done for him. But He who created both of them, the DOG and the MAN, as well as those people who saw that poor dog in its miserable condition and did not trouble themselves, knows and values.

جمله معشوق است و عاشق پرده ای

Everyone is created free, granted a life free, and his needs are secured free, as such each and every person is freely welcome to join and to serve others if he feels and wishes. This service is a simple appreciation and it is to show the devotee's surrender to the Most High. The amount of service is not the aim, it is the sincerity that matters and is valued.

A Darvish is a person who appears to live as any other member of human family. He lives, works, enjoys, serves and gets his necessities by honest work and service in the same way any other honest person has to secure his life requirements. The only exception is the amount of extra effort and intention his heart puts into his work to prepare a better environment, better happier and healthier life for others as well as himself.

The Darvish believes that the soul is bestowed upon him from Hagh, and thus it is his duty to live as Hagh expects him to live, to think as Hagh, to serve as Hagh, to give a Hagh and know he is as an illusion in a mirror reflecting Hagh to this world. He is nobody, owns nothing, has nothing, desires nothing, wishes nothing, and is nothing at all but in the meantime he is so precious since he is a true image of the light of Hagh.

A Sufi or Darvish believes that since everybody's ROOH—Spirit—is from HAGH, everybody is representative of HAGH, and so everybody deserves his sincere SERVICE perfectly.

خلاف طريقت بود كاولياء

It is contrary to the Path of truth if the lovers

تمنا كنند از خدا جز خدا

Ask the beloved (God) for anything but God (Himself)

گر از دوست چشمت بر احسان اوست

If your anticipation from beloved is His favour

تو در بند خويشی نه در بند دوست

You are in your own captivity you are not in His love

Saadi

Abu Saeed the great Sufi Master of all times, was once asked by someone Abu Saeed which is the shortest way to Hagh? He replied:

"Securing comfort for others."

On another occasion he said:

"Generosity is to give, before being asked."

Abol Hassan Kharaghaani, the great fifth century A.H. Darvish and the Master and Teacher of Abu Saeed, did not lay any condition of gender or sex, race, religion, colour, friend or enemy for serving the person who needed help. If a person needed help, was sick, newly arrived to the neighborhood, a stranger, an old prominent member of society, a close friend, or anybody else, that person was to be served. He commanded his followers and disciples:

"Whoever enters these gates SERVE him but DO NOT ask about his name and belief."

جمله معشوق است و عاشق پرده ای

And He also said:

"Scientists when they wake up to start their day they wish for more knowledge. Ascetics desire more asceticism, while Abol Hassan is captive to how he may prepare happiness in the heart of a brother."

حق یکی و عشق حق یکی , خلقت حق بخشایشی است از روح وحدانیت حق همه مخلوق حضرت حق را,

HAGH is ONE His LOVE is ONE and all of His creatures are bestowed by His ONE SOUL.

ایشان همه تلولو نور الهی را گوئی در آینه ها نشر میدهند

They all are manifestations of His light as the reflections of light in different mirrors.

Hazrate Ghadeer Ali Shah

جمله معشوق است و عاشق پرده ای

THE WORLD IS A MIRROR REFLECTING
CHARACTER AND PERSONALITY

The sincere Darvish is the one who thinks positively, he sees beauty, he loves beauty and he experiences beauty. Sufis believe that if someone sees or experiences anything imperfect, improper, faulty, ugly or wrong, it is the one with this perception who is to be blamed for the imperfection in his eye and mind.

A Darvish believes that he must remind himself that he himself is not A Complete Man. It is better for him to recall his imperfection before any judgment of others. How may such an imperfect person judge another person? How can he point his judgmental finger towards their imperfection? If he is tempted, the Darvish must stop and repent from his misjudgment.

People are like roses, a rose is beautiful in colour and appearance, lovely in scent, but this gorgeous rose always has thorns on the stem. A rose lover never sees those thorns but accepts them as part of the rose. To this person the rose is a combination of all of those qualities and properties, the rose's beauty is in all of those parts combined, and even the thorns are beautiful in their own way.

A Sufi sister was listening to one of her friends, another Darvish, complaining to her about a crow living amongst the tall trees in her garden.

"This ugly, big crow starts singing at all times of the day, making such an ugly, terrible, ear-scratching noise. I can hardly stand it anymore."

The Sufi sister smiled, "What a beautiful Zekr this crow is reciting."

Her friend was surprised, "What Zekr is that, I do not understand?"

جمله معشوق است و عاشق پرده ای

"Listen carefully, and pay more attention to get the message. You must become familiar with the crow's pronunciation; don't you see it says HAGH, HAGH, HAGH?"

Her friend paused for short time and then she said, "Oh yes, yes it is true the crow is reciting Zekr, and it is saying Hagh." She clasped her friend's hand," Thank you for opening my mind, and thank you for drawing my attention to reality and not leaving me alone with my imagination."

To a Sufi the world around him is a mirror reflecting his character and personality, if he sees something unpleasant it is his duty for him to look into his mind and heart for the reason and wisely eliminate his own sin there. He is not to blame other people, but to blame himself.

To a Darvish everything happening to him is proper, it occurs for a reason, the reason which is not known to him at the time. Therefore, if something is not agreeable to his ego and passion he has no right to follow his instincts and condemn, it is better for him to accept it with a smile upon his lips, waiting patiently until the time the reason becomes known to him.

WHAT IS THE DESTINATION OF THE MAN

WHO IS SO HASTY AND SPEEDY?

From time immemorial in Khaneghaah the Darvishes have as a principal part of their work ethic, one simple model for life:

I for you; You for anyone you wish

They believe this is the message of the real and true humanity. It is for all; everyone who feels the invitation for service and love.

Darvishes have their ear to the commands of those who invite and persuade them to serve:

❖ Love others and give them privilege over yourself.

❖ Give and grant without any expectation for reward

To Darvishes the sun is one of the best visible examples of giving freely, and they do practice the example. See how the sun spreads out its rays of light and warmth to the whole world without any expectation for appreciation?

The world today is an unbelievably tumultuous and delirious story of progress in sciences and technology. Man is aggressively speeding towards modern and fresh achievements, ideas, new opinions and perceived exciting modern techniques while sadly and regrettably being unaware of the fact that he is leaving behind the traditional and seemingly outdated. The more modern his life, he has the impression that a modern life is the most charming, everything appearing to be beautiful. But in spite of all of those superficial attractions Man's life—with the same speed—is going towards depression, personal problems, less mutual respect, less mutual understanding, less confidence in each other, less honesty and less forgiveness and a more complex sense of fragile hollowness.

جمله معشوق است و عاشق پرده ای

What type of life is it going to be in the future?

What is the destination of the man who is so hasty and speedy? Is he aiming for self-destruction? To the majority of people the material life appears to be more comfortable and in many ways easier, but in spite of that despite the outward glamour and beauty, the same man has found himself lonelier in himself. He has to work longer hours generally but also work overtime, sometimes in menial jobs and under poor conditions, only for a so called easier and more luxurious environment.

Because of all of the continuous rush and rush this modern person does not have enough time for proper food or to have a family meeting, family talks, agreements, disputes, happiness and pleasant or unpleasant times that make a man a true man, a real human. All of those pressures, discomforts, and restlessness will cause him to seek refuge in caffeine, drugs, alcohol and so many other artificial stimulants to keep him awake and give him the very temporary power to be able to have extra time needed to spend on work or consequent sufferings.

To achieve easy money, some people think they are smart and get themselves involved in any number of destructive and dishonest business transactions which will lead them in the final utmost stages of self-destruction to either prison or psychiatric hospitals. All of these are only the worldly and material consequences, the moral consequences and punishment of the heart is a much higher matter.

Man finds himself cornered under such heavy, fierce pressures and gradually feels the consequences. He feels he has no choice except to create a transparent but thick and unbreakable shell around himself. This man becomes tired, bad tempered, aggressive, with no sense of humor, loses his appetite, and becomes hasty and even merciless. He thinks nothing can help him at this stage and he draws himself back to shelter inside his shell; a shell produced from his impatience, lack of love, suspicion and lack of confidence. The fact is that he makes himself alone and then becomes lonely, to him it appears that he is similar to a silk worm, imprisoned in his cocoon which does not leave him any power to break through this shell of loneliness and solitude, and in the course of time he gradually loses any interest or intention to break through that shell at all.

It is obvious that in such a critical situation the man is in need of true treatment and real medicine, he needs something to dissolve that shell and solve his problem. He needs to understand that the physician is his heart and the medicine he needs is love; a love somehow new and different from his previous presumption of love.

But just as any other person addicted to drugs, alcohol or gambling this wounded, damaged and cheated man of today does not agree, believe or accept that such love exists. Would it be easy for him to accept and agree with this system of love which is true and honest? The love which is poured on him is a love without any expectation for return or favour in exchange, it is the magic medicine to all of his sickness.

To this victim of time and circumstances, an innocent system of devotion and giving without wanting is unbelievable and unacceptable. When compared to his existing materialistic way of life where everything is given a material value and giving and not expecting to receive it is seen as strange, unbelievable and unacceptable. To this person even hearing about someone who is offering free help creates lots of difficult questions and suspicions. Because of his experience and the way of questioning it is normal that the person turns down the offering hands extended to him, despite the love and readiness to help. The person who is dying to receive some help and love believes it would not be possible. Alas, alas what a disaster! What a loss!

How could it be possible to convince somebody with bitter experiences that there also exists someone who is ready to render love freely, without any reasoning and expectation and ask of nothing in exchange? A Darvish in Khaneghaah not only is guided and taught but also through experience learns ways to convince him that contrary to his past experiences yes such devotion and such rich emotion does exist, and is happily and sincerely available to him as well. A devoted Darvish has the duty to render true happiness to our all people who suffer the troubles as the above sad man.

This seems to be strange to the man of our times, but it is a real fact and reality. It is the goal and duty for Darvishes and to them it not only exists but is truly alive. Darvishes are trained to prove this reality and this beauty in their actions; not just in saying the nice words, but by DOING IT.

Darvishes in Khaneghaah feel the reality that exists in this simple sentence "I for you" and Darvishes are directed carefully, step-by-step to investigate, study and feel in his heart and mind to go through the benefits and the results achievable from this action.

جمله معشوق است و عاشق پرده ای

The teaching of Khaneghaah to the Darvishes is to have faith constructed on LOVE, DEVOTION and SERVICE, without any hope for recognition or eye on wages, rewards, social recognition or thanks giving of any kind.

In Khaneghaah an ordinary man with all of the qualities of both good and bad registers and practices truly and honestly through his heart the Khaneghaah's teaching and trainings. Let us assume and let us think in a material way and see what will happen if that aim is followed?

When someone comes to a person and offers him his totally sincere service and devotion and tells him that: I for you, I ignore my personal selfish desires for your sake. Please permit me to serve you.

And then;

On the same basis as the above, the second person goes to another person who is devastated and offers him the same as what has been offered to him, and then the third person does the same offering to the next person; what will happen? What will the change in human society be? What will it be changed or turned into? Doesn't it seem that all of us are investing in such a great love and devotion Bank which continually gives and distributes amongst the needy any amount of love they require and need irrespective of whether they apply for it or not?

This Bank will be the only Bank in the history of Mankind where it's capital, in spite of all of those payments and all of its expenses, and irrespective of the fact that it does not charge any interest or working expenses, that not only does it not reduce from the capital, but the capital becomes bigger and bigger every day, and after each and every transaction. In fact this Bank is not giving it is a receiving Bank. The reserves of LOVE are unlimited.

Wouldn't the whole world become a real paradise? The paradise which of course does not contain palaces built of gold and silver, or trees of emeralds, or fruits of diamonds, or rubies. Wouldn't it be a paradise full of happy people?

When I ignore and disregard my material desires I travel away from 'I', out of 'I', and reach YOU; and You in the same way travel out of your 'I', for the sake of your' YOU', the results stretch to infinity.

A Sufi is taught in Khaneghaah to observe the world from that high position, to observe the reality of Hagh's Creation, thus he observes Hagh has created the sun for the benefit of His creatures, so that the sun extends out its rays of light and warmth to all and everyone freely and equally. The Darvish notes the soft light of the moon and the twinkling of the stars, twinkling during the night times in dark wide and quiet oceans of sky, and he thinks about how Hagh sends clouds to rain and to water the plants and all other creatures. He even goes further and humbly and with gratitude sees how Hagh has bestowed from his Soul into Man. Then the Darvish comes to feel and understand the reality that he himself is a high creature of God, and with an unlimited amount of HAGH's favour upon him and all of His Creation.

With this idea the Darvish discovers how great the responsibility he has to provide sincere loving service and to act sincerely and lovingly towards others is. All of this comes to him and touches his heart since he has consulted his heart sincerely and used his mind, taking the benefit of wisdom and directing all thoughts towards the path to Truth and sincerity. All of those heartfelt achievements are consequences of what he has been and are now directed forwards in the course of the training in Khaneghaah. Khaneghaah takes a raw uncooked man, cooks, and trains and changes him to become a servant of creation.

In order to give and serve, to offer freely and not to expect any reward a person has to free himself from limits and boundaries created by him and his kind. But to be free Man has to break the chains of ego, selfishness, pride and the desire of self-advantage above others. To reach that high position one must be selfless; he must evaporate all of his material wishes. Man has to be completely dissolved in the love of Hagh. In fact he must die out of himself and become born again in LOVE.

A Darvish must live accordingly, if not he has the title but not the quality. This transformation does not seem to be easy, but even more than that, looks like being impossible. Ego does not want to leave and does not permit man to get rid of it. In Khaneghaah Darvish find the way to do the impossible, to reduce the ego to a minimum and control it to the maximum.

In Khaneghaah a Darvish is directed to feel with his heart and soul that to love others and to give love is the start of taking one step out of the self. By taking that one step out of the self he must leave behind him all of comfort self has in living inside the self-centering, and must save himself from the satisfaction he gets from being in love with himself. Khaneghaah is the place where a Darvish sits sincerely

جمله معشوق است و عاشق پرده ای

with himself and truly decides to take the first step out of selfishness. This first step is too heavy, too difficult, and so painful to make it happen by himself, but this place—The Khaneghaah—is where it makes it possible for him to ignore the entire heavy load of pain and sadness that may appear to him. No matter how long it takes, true love is contained in the first step out of self, moving towards serving and loving the next person.

After this first heavy step is taken and Man has come out from under his shell of selfishness, ego, self-centering and desires, he will see how glorious and beautiful the world of serving others is and he will be a completely new man living in the same old body.

When Baa Yazeed (The great Persian Darvish) was asked "Who is a Darvish", he replied:

"The one who discovers in the deepest part of his heart the greatest treasure, and finds in there the gracious most expensive jewel of LOVE, such a person is a Darvish."

In some cases a Sufi may feel that he falls short, or is incapable, or not strong enough to solve other people's problems. It may happen at the beginning when he feels separate to the person. Khaneghaah warns Darvishes of being different from others and not to feel separation from other members of their society. A Darvish is a positive charitable servant of his society in particular and to Mankind in general. By surrendering the false image of separateness and to see Unity he will then conduct his actions through love and show his sincere desire to render heartfelt sympathy; the span of his arms will then feel to be as wide as the whole world. His flow of love seems to be capable of opening to the person in need the gates of the largest rose garden of happiness and hope.

A Darvish believes love is in unity and not separation, love is in having heartfelt feelings for others and not ignoring them, love is in service without expectation of any recognition and of acknowledgment. Love does not break, but it repairs all that is broken, love does not forget but remembers and reminds; love is to suffer and bear the pain on behalf of someone who is suffering from any pain, with the hope and intention of relieving misery; love is also sharing the joy and happiness with someone who wishes to share good times and occasions with a friend.

A Darvish goes to Khaneghaah to forget himself, his thoughts, wishes, interests and existence to become ONE with his Beloved, to become one with the whole universe. Anyone who goes to Khaneghaah, but does not realise these qualities must of course, according to his capacity, search inside his heart and mind for that weakness, whatever is at fault, and find a proper sincere cure.

A Darvish knows that he is not the main reason for the whole of Creation, a stupid idea which is a byproduct of ego and self-centering. In contrast, his wish is to feel that he is nothing and his passion and contents do not exist. A Darvish observes the whole of Creation according to his capacity. He intends to understand the secrets of Creation and to rise above all of them. Surprisingly he finds a lot of reasons that are beyond the understanding of his capacity and nature. It is evident that different people have different capacities and so their understandings differ accordingly.

To all nave Darvishes the Khaneghaah teaches that since the whole of Creation is from Hagh, the Darvish must love each and every one of the creatures, without any expectation for return of the favour, or judgment of the creature receiving this valuable love.

As for a nave Darvish the message of Sufism to the Man of today is quite simple but constructive:

- ❖ Travel out of yourself, out of your I and go towards another you (to you)

- ❖ Observe the results of this pure and gracious travel out of your self

- ❖ You will feel this ladder assists you to arrive at the wide gates of Mercy and Love

- ❖ When you arrive to this high position everyone will appear to you as pure, lovable and innocent as they are in the eye of HAGH

- ❖ You understand that all people are deserving of your sincere love and consequent services without any expectation in return.

Sarry e Saghaty lived for ninety eight years d. 245 or 250 A.H. and has many maxims and teachings providing advice on the subject of "Love for God and Monotheism": He says

جمله معشوق است و عاشق پرده ای

- ❖ A Gnostic shines on the whole world in the same way as the sun does.

- ❖ A Gnostic carries all the load of good as well as the burdens of bad the same way as the earth does.

- ❖ A Gnostic is the liquid soul of life for all hearts in the same way as water is for the life of all creatures.

- ❖ A Gnostic bestows his warmth and light on all of the people the same way as fire does for people.

حق یکی و عشق حق یکی , خلقت حق بخشایشی است از روح وحدانیت حق همه مخلوق حضرت حق را,

HAGH is ONE His LOVE is ONE and all of His creatures are bestowed by His ONE SOUL.

ایشان همه تلولو نور الهی را گونی در آینه ها نشر میدهند

They all are manifestations of His light as the reflections of light in different mirrors.

Hazrate Ghadeer Ali Shah

جمله معشوق است و عاشق پرده ای

GLOSSARY

Darvish	Sufi
Doost	Friend and beloved
Faghr	Personal qualities of meekness and indigence
Hazrate	Holy
Hagh	Allah, God, Jehovah, Ahoora Mazda, Yahweh
Jesm	Physical existence
Jesmaani	Physical
Khaneghaah	Gathering place
Khane ye Khooda	House of God
Peer	Teacher
Maktab e Tasavvof	Maktab (School) e (of) Tasavvof (Sufism)
Morshed	Spiritual Guide
Nave Darvish	Unregistered student of Sufism
Rooh	Soul
Roohaani	Spiritual
Samaa	Dance
Selseleh	Sufi Order
Seyr	Conscience
Sheykh	Head of the Sufi Order
Solook	Outward manifest behaviour
Zoroaster	Founding Persian Prophet of Zoroastrianism

جمله معشوق است و عاشق پرده ای

RECOMMENDED READING

Islam

It is recommended by the author that Western readers who are interested in reading the Qur'an (Koran) discover the historical context before attempting it.

"Islam—A Short History", "Muhammad—A Biography of The Prophet" and **"The Bible—The Biography"**
Karen Armstrong, Phoenix

"After The Prophet—The Epic Story of the Shia-Sunni Split"
Lesley Hazelton, Anchor Books

"The Koran"
Translated from the Arabic by J.M. Rodwell, Phoenix.

Sufism
Moulana Rumi
Saadi

"The Green Sea of Heaven—Fifty Ghazals from the Diwan of Hafiz"
Translated by Elizabeth T Gray Jr, White Cloud Press, Oregon

"When You Think of Hoofbeats Think of a Zebra"
Shems Friedlander, Harper and Row

"Love Poems From God—Twelve Voices from the East and West"
Daniel Ladinsky, Penguin Compass

جمله معشوق است و عاشق پرده ای